LIFE FROM
A NEW ANGLE

A Journey of Faith

Allan J. Bowers

Every rich blessing.
Allan

Alpha Publishing

First published in Great Britain in 2005 by
Alpha Publishing

Copies may be obtained from:

Allan J. Bowers
Treetops
25 Woolbrook Park
Sidmouth
Devon
EX10 9DX

British Library Cataloguing in Publication Data

A C.I.P. for this book is available from the British Library

ISBN 0-9549808-0-8

Designed, edited, typeset and produced by The Studio Publishing Services Ltd, 4A Brookside Units, Venny Bridge, Exeter EX4 8JN

Contents

To my wife Betty, a partner in my work and inspiration in the faith whose love and care have been constant, and in memory of my parents

List of Illustrations

Front cover: Life from a new angle
Back cover: Author's portrait

List of Illustrations

Foreword

Ministry, preaching, painting, poetry, hymn writing, wood carving and music have been the joy of my life. Those who love these art forms know that they only reflect a portion of one's life. The rest of my life has kept on an even keel by my belief in God's existence, and his revelation of the meaning of life in Jesus Christ whose teaching is so striking, so original, so full of mystery and so illuminating. Writing this autobiography has helped me to get things in perspective, to see my life as a microcosm of something larger. Virginia Woolf said: "If life has a base it is in memory". I trust that by allowing memory to hold the door, what I have written about my journey of faith may be of interest not only to my family and friends but to those who desire to be part of the great "Society of Explorers" seeking the meaning of life and in doing so to find the precious gift of joy.

Allan J. Bowers
Sidmouth

Introduction and Acknowledgements

My reason for writing this autobiography was chiefly for my family and friends, but also for readers interested in thinking about life as a pilgrimage of faith.

I wish to place on record my thanks to the Imperial War Museum in London and the Museum of Army Chaplaincy in Amport for accepting a record of my service as an Army Chaplain in Hong Kong and Korea.

My book is a record of the life of a minister in the Methodist Church spanning almost sixty years, telling of some of my experiences and providing me with an opportunity to thank all who have supported and worked with me in ministry.

I feel constrained to thank by name the following. My father, who before he died sent me a potted history of members of our family and many letters describing life in the army during the First World War. My brother and sisters for their interest in my work as a minister. But I especially wish to thank my dear wife, a partner in work and an encourager and inspiration in the faith, whose love and support have been constant as she has shared with me in my ministry all the time we have been together.

I am also grateful to my friend, Dr Patricia Batstone, who showed me how to prepare a manuscript for publication, and to the Reverend Gerald Burt, M.A. for reading the first draft and giving much time and expertise in advising on the format of my manuscript.

To my nephew, Oliver Heid: thanks for the cover design, illustrating the power of angles and light, and thanks to Mr David Miller of The Studio Publishing Services Ltd, for his ready help in designing and typesetting the book.

Finally, thanks to the *Methodist Recorder* for permission to print material contained in their newspaper, and to the Epworth Press for a quotation from the book *The Path to Perfection* by the Reverend Dr W. Edwin Sangster.

Allan J. Bowers

Chapter One

Family, Home, and Church

My first clear memory of life was at the age of four running round the living room of our London home naked, much to the amusement of my parents. It was a perfectly innocent thing but the event stands out in my memory because for the first time I became aware that I was alive, and like a young lamb frolicking on the grass I experienced a carefree joy. Joy had invaded my life.

I was born on April 2nd 1923 at 68 Mildenhall Road, Clapton, in the Borough of Hackney, where my parents lived in three rooms let out to them as a temporary arrangement by a kind friend whom I was taught to call "Auntie Edie". At that time there was a dearth of accommodation in London and much deprivation and unemployment. Auntie Edie was present at my birth and consented to be my godmother. She was also present at my baptism at the Anglican church, St James-the-Less, Bethnal Green. Soon after my birth we moved to a large house in Clapton that was owned by my grandfather Bowers, where there was plenty of accommodation for my parents, my elder brother, Stanley, and my sister, Hilda. It was in this house that Grace, my younger sister, was born.

The house next door was also owned by my grandfather, where he lived with my grandmother and their daughter, Auntie Lilly, and her husband, Uncle Frank, and their three children, Percy, Leonard, and Irene. We were close and happy families.

Left to right: Stanley, Allan and Hilda

My mother had four children, all within the space of four years. We had no problems in playing together because in those days we had to make our own entertainment, there being no radio and television.

My father, Percival William Bowers, was born on the 7th July, 1890 at Dunlace Road, Clapton. After a formal education he became a journalist on a London newspaper, the *Star and Morning Leader*, but in 1907 he left the career of journalism to enlist in the 7th Battalion, The Royal Fusiliers, as a cadet. On completing his drills he joined the King's Own Royal Lancaster Regiment and served with them for one year in Lancaster and Jersey and later in South Africa.

Just before the outbreak of the First World War, my father transferred to the 12th Royal Lancers, and on 16th of August 1914, on a beautiful Sunday morning, saw the 12th Royal Lancers and their 680 horses making for Thorpe Railway Station for the boxing of the horses and their journey on to Southampton. They landed at Le Havre on a Monday morning and proceeded to the front line and their first engagement in the Great War. My father was present at the battle of Mons, and stood behind the gun of "E" Battery, which fired the first shots on land in France. The battle was horrendous and many thousands of soldiers were killed. For my father this baptism of fire was a traumatic experience that scarred him for the rest of his life, even though he escaped injury. The horror of that particular battle, for which he was awarded the Mons Star with a clasp inscribed "August 14th to November 14th", he never talked about to us children. It is a merciful thing that so often memory becomes dull and such experiences are pushed deep down into the subconscious mind, never to be retrieved, but sometimes to affect future health and happiness.

From my father's notes on his wartime experiences I gather that there were long rides, nearly always in a circle at night. Most of the days were spent in cornfields, feeding their horses. There were very many skirmishes with the enemy and on one day he records that he was on an advanced patrol with four other men and one officer. They had been told by the French civilians that the Germans had spent the night in their village and some were thought to be still there. Father moved slowly on his horse, expecting any moment to be fired at, when a corporal shouted that a Death's Head Hussar officer from the far end of the village was coming towards them at great speed. They all opened fire and the horse was wounded but somehow the German managed to escape. Father galloped down the side entrance of a house, over a garden wall, and saw a number of Germans retreating with pennants flying. He fired several shots but they got away, later to be captured by the Dragoon Guards.

German cavalry, vanguards in their many thousands, were in retreat after the battle of Mons. Father kept with his regiment throughout the war and went in and out of those dreaded trenches with his Commanding Officer and Adjutant until late 1915, when he was sent to the General Headquarters 3rd Echelon, Rouen. There he was billeted with a French family for nine months until, in May

1919, he was recalled to Cologne to rejoin his regiment. He remained in Cologne for two weeks and then returned home to England for demobilization. On the 19th May 1919 he entered the War Office in London, and remained there for thirty-six years, as a clerical officer. In 1919 life was very hard for many ex-soldiers, though father was well provided for with his War Office work. There were long queues outside all the Labour Exchanges; the dole at that time was only ten shillings a week, and there were no family allowances or National Assistance.

My mother, Dorothy Ethel Bowers, née Mogg, was born on the 22nd August 1897. Father first met her in the summer of 1913, at a party given by his mother to celebrate his safe return from service in

Mother and Father – Clacton-on-Sea, August 1936

South Africa. Dorothy was only sixteen, but it was love at first sight, although they did not meet again until December 1914, when, because they were so much in love, they decided to write to each other every few days through the war. They became engaged in January 1918 and were married on 16th March 1918 at St James-the-Less Anglican Church, Bethnal Green, the church in which she was baptized and worshipped as a teenager, and which she loved.

I knew father and mother loved each other dearly because I often saw them cuddle. Father told me that when he first met her she had deep brown curly hair in long tresses, but unfortunately, during the great influenza epidemic of 1919, she became so ill that she lost all her curls.

Mother was a most attractive woman. She had brown eyes, was quite tall and had a loving and caring nature. She was a homemaker and very house proud; all the furniture was highly polished, down to the fire grate in the living room where we had our meals. Mother excelled in making our house a home where we felt secure and happy. Eighty-one Elderfield Road, Clapton, where we lived, was built on what was once a field of elder trees, situated about a mile from the river Lea, which flowed through Hackney marshes. The garden was surrounded by a high brick wall. As a boy I was most imaginative; wonderland was imported into our garden, which, though long and narrow, I transformed in my mind into a beautiful park with lawns that swept down to a reed-edged lake. The house consisted of two floors, a basement, and a passage to the cellar, which I thought of as a dungeon. When there was torrential rain the drain outside the scullery overflowed and formed a moat in the lower part of the garden. I imagined that I was king of the castle, and used to sing the nursery rhyme to my younger sister, Grace: "I'm king of the castle, get down you dirty rascal!" Of course, it was only play-ful fun, we got on so well together.

My elder sister, Hilda, was studious, and spent a great deal of time in her bedroom studying. She said she recalled seeing me shuffle around on the floor on my bottom, with one leg tucked underneath the other, because I was late in learning to walk. Mother used to complain that my clothes got very dirty as a result of this means of locomotion.

Mother was an excellent cook, and though money was scarce we all had plenty to eat. Father had passed all his Civil Service examinations and his occupation at the War Office was secure. The wages were small, a little over £2 a week to keep themselves and four growing children. Fortunately, he only paid a low rent to his father for the house, and repaired all our shoes, which he cut out in leather from a pattern and used a last on which to nail the leather to the shoes. Mother was clever with a needle and had a Singer sewing machine on which she made all my sisters' dresses and coats. Monday was always washday, which I hated. The copper in the corner of the scullery was lit before breakfast and soon the house smelt of washing and soap suds. With astonishing energy mother had all the clothes washed and the water squeezed out of them by passing them through the rollers of the iron mangle, which I loved to turn. The clothes were hung on a line in the garden to dry and then neatly folded. I loved the clean, fresh-air smell of the clothes. Mother hated washdays when it rained, because the clothes took so long to dry indoors and she was a stickler for them being well aired.

Monday lunch usually was bubble and squeak and the remains of the Sunday joint. If it was beef we all enjoyed dripping sandwiches at tea-time, made succulent with a sprinkling of salt. On Monday evenings Uncle Cameron, a science teacher at Bethnal Green Grammar School, came to tea and afterwards played billiards in the parlour upstairs. An upright piano stood there and sometimes mother would play it. I played a game called "Church" with my sister, Grace. She was the congregation and I was the preacher. We would get some kind of music from the piano. Little did I realize that one day I would become a preacher.

I remember the day father proudly brought home a gramophone, "His Master's Voice" The first record he played was called "The Laughing Policeman", which made *us* laugh until our sides ached.

I had a magic lantern given to me, and I used to give shows to my brother and sisters. It wasn't until much later that we had wireless. We had only gas lights, and I remember the lamp lighter coming down the road when it was dusk, lighting the gas lamps in the street with his long pole. It always fascinated me to watch him lift the pole high and light the lamp. In these days of clean air and smokeless fuel it's hard to imagine what a London fog was like. We called them "pea-soupers". The wintry months would bring acrid fogs. The air was so thick and yellow that one could hardly see where one was going. The old trams would be bumper to bumper from Hackney to Bethnal Green. Shipping came to a standstill on the river Thames. People suffering from bronchitis and asthma, especially babies, often died. What a relief it was when the fog dispersed and the sun shone to make things normal again.

Most of the shopping was bought in Chatsworth Road, near where we lived. Market day brought lots of people out looking for bargains. Outside A. H. Toms eel and pie shop were rows of steel trays on folding tables containing different sizes of wriggling eels. It fascinated me just to watch them, and then a customer would point out the eel he wanted and Mr. Toms, dressed in a blue and white shiny apron, would pick it up and place it on a wooden board dripping with the blood of previous eels, chop its head off, and cut the wriggling body into pieces and wrap it up for the customer. Not far away was an old woman standing at a salt stall, cutting up large blocks of salt at about 2 lbs for a halfpenny, and there was another woman grating horse-radish at one or two pennies a bag. Cat lovers could purchase red raw horse meat for their pet's food.

I often stood outside Watford and Taylor's horse funerals, watching through an open door a carpenter making coffins. A funeral procession in those days was always a sight. Usually there were four black horses to pull the hearse and a carriage following pulled by two horses. Mr Watford, immaculately dressed and wearing a black top hat, walked in front of the hearse, and as it passed by everyone stood still and men took off their hats as a mark of respect.

I have a vivid memory of the barber's shop because mother would send me for a haircut, which had to be cut "short back and sides". After he had finished cutting my hair it looked like a prison crop, and I really felt shorn. I remember that it cost about two pence.

Not far from our house was a sweet shop and on the way to school when I had my penny a week pocket money, I would take pleasure in buying four farthings' worth of sweets, usually brandy balls, or white peppermint sticks, which looked like chalk. There was also a lucky dip, which I had to pay a penny for, and more often than not the lucky dip proved abortive!

I had a religious upbringing, Sunday was always a special day in our house. My parents sent us children to Sunday School, always dressed in our best clothes. We had to change before dinner and put our best clothes on again for afternoon Sunday School. We were not allowed to play games on Sundays. My Sunday School teacher, Mrs Irene Juniper, was a wonderful story teller. She made the Bible characters come alive and spoke about Jesus as if he were her daily companion, without whom life would be inconceivable. If we listened carefully to the Bible story she promised that for the last ten minutes she would read to us from Richmal Crompton's *Just William*, which simply enthralled me as William was a character with whom I could identify. Every week I left Sunday School looking forward to the next Sunday's *Just William* story: at that time, although I liked Mrs Juniper's Bible stories, they didn't grip me.

The church became the centre of life because, as we were without wireless and there was no television, we had to make our own entertainment, much of which was provided by the church. In addition to my one penny a week pocket money mother let me have *Hotspur*, a magazine for boys.

When I had just turned eight, my sister Hilda contracted yellow jaundice. Soon after I also became ill, and though I did not know it at the time, jaundice was to affect my health for years to come. I remember seeing discolouration of my skin and feeling very ill. It seemed an age before I felt better. I had lost some weight and my parents thought it would be good for me to go on convalescence into the country, to a place arranged by our doctor. I was told that it would be like going on holiday and that I would be with children of my own age. I am sure that my parents thought it would build me up in health and that I would be very happy. How mistaken they were: in fact it was a period of my childhood when I felt most miserable. Mother packed a case for me and we went by train to a place in the country called Carshalton. I didn't cry, but when mother left me in that strange place I thought I would never see her again. Matron was a big woman who never seemed to smile, and I discovered her to be cruel. I felt homesick from the start. Matron was not a bit like my wonderful mother. If a boy was naughty she would hold the child's head and hit him under the chin with her knuckled fist several times until he cried. I wanted to report her, but I was afraid that I would get the knuckle treatment and so I was always on my best behaviour. We were allowed to write home and secretly I thought I would escape, but never plucked up the courage. After all, I was only eight! Days turned into weeks and it seemed like an eternity, but one wonderful day the matron told me I was going home the next day and I could pack my case. The next day was the most wonderful day of my life. I never wanted to see the place again. I couldn't wait to get home.

I soon went back to school and joined the Cubs at our local church. Life again was full of fun and joy. I had to be careful not to eat fatty foods and I remember having some bad bilious attacks, mostly at night when my father would put his arms around me and hold me tight. Stomach-aches often affected me, but as I grew older they seemed to disappear. I enjoyed all the activities of the Cubs, and each year the Scouts put on a "Gang Show" arranged by Ralph Reader, who was a friend of the scoutmaster. The songs were popular and one I especially liked was "We're riding along on the crest of the wave and the sun is in the sky". One year I was asked to sing a song entitled "Round about the age of me", my stage debut. I was terrified; it was my first taste of being on a stage in front of a packed hall, but somehow I liked it.

One thing I always looked forward to was the visit of the chimney sweep. He came once a year to sweep our living room chimney and the fireplaces on the two floors above it. He wore an old felt cap and carried a large bag of equipment. The furniture in the living room was covered with dustsheets; everything had been made ready for him. He fitted his rods together, on the first of which there was a circular brush, and as the sweep pushed the brush up the chimney he asked me to go out into the garden and tell him when the brush appeared through the chimney pot. When I saw it I gave him a sign and he then pushed the brush up and down until the soot fell down into the bag made ready, and when I returned his face and hands were covered with soot. He looked a pretty picture and I couldn't help laughing. Some years later, at a Sunday School anniversary, a visiting speaker asked us children to show our hands, and so the school of over a hundred children held up their hands and he said: "You can't go to heaven if you have dirty hands." My mind went back to the sweep with his dirty hands. The speaker quoted a verse from Psalm 24: "Who shall ascend the hill of the Lord and who shall stand in his holy place? He who has clean hands and a pure heart". I felt sure that God would welcome the sweep with his sooty hands into heaven. Mother's hands were often dirty but I knew she would go to heaven.

I also recall my first Greek lesson at a Sunday School anniversary, when a distinguished minister, Reverend Dr Newton Flew told us the Greek word for "worthy"! "All say after me, 'Worthy'", and then he gave us the Greek word, *akseeos*, which we had to shout out at the top of our voices. It is interesting how these experiences from childhood often stay with us and years later we remember them. But not all experiences are happy ones. One night I awoke to see a spider on the sleeve of my pyjamas. I got out of bed and let out a scream that brought my father to see what was wrong. He quickly disposed of the creature, but I still have a dislike of spiders. I also remember running down the stairs from the front door and, unable to stop myself, hitting my forehead against the armchair, knocking myself out for a few seconds and then discovering a pool of blood on the floor. The wound required several stitches and on my first passport was: "distinguishing mark – scar over right eye".

I had a vivid imagination, and when I heard that my grandmother Mogg believed herself to be related to King Haakon, my imagination ran wild. Could I possibly be a prince? A film entitled *The Prince and the Pauper*, which I really enjoyed, only fed my imagination. This story was about a young boy, the image of a prince, who, by mutual agreement changed places with the real prince and entered a new world. For months after seeing the film I imagined I was a prince, but came down to earth as the picture in my mind gradually faded and once more I lived, not in a palace but at 81 Elderfield Road.

In those days I went regularly to the cinema. I fell in love, and out of love, with many of the film stars, Clark Gable, Errol Flynn, Spencer Tracy, Humphrey Bogart, and Shirley Temple, to name but a few. I adored Walt Disney's cartoons, especially the animated figure of Mickey Mouse, who made his debut in 1928 when I was five, and Popeye whose muscles became as strong as steel by eating spinach. Grace, my younger sister, often went with me to the cinema and when not at the cinema we went to our local church's uniformed organizations. We also went to The Band of Hope, a strong temperance meeting. I recall seeing men and women leave a public house near where we lived drunk and incapable. It was one of the reasons why, at an early age, I signed the temperance certificate.

At Junior School I was introduced to drawing and painting. The art teacher encouraged me in drawing and I enjoyed his classes so much that my bedroom became my studio. I thought that one day I would be like Rembrandt, a renowned painter. I don't think I was very religious, but attendance at Sunday School and church gradually awakened my mind and I became a regular attender at church services. The organist introduced me to the world of music and philosophy. We would go for long walks on Chingford plains, when we talked about the meaning of life and discussed such questions as "What is mind and matter?"; "Has the universe a purpose?"; "Has my life a purpose?"; "Where does God fit into all of this?"; "Where did I come from?"; and "Where am I going?" I also used to pump the organ behind a curtain, following a gauge, but sometimes I didn't pump hard enough and the organ began to make funny noises and then I would quicken the pace. I enjoyed all these activities.

As I have mentioned, my elder sister Hilda was studious. My brother, Stanley, was a thinker. I had an ordinary education, primary and junior school, and then Upton House Central School on Urswick Road, Hackney, which had a laboratory and a small indoor swimming pool. It was an old Victorian building, and at one time had been a Borstal. The assembly hall and playground were large. I remember some names: Captain Allard, the headmaster, and sweet Mr Thomas, the French master, who had a bulbous nose. One day at a lesson he said: "Bowers, what is the French for nose?" I couldn't give the word, whereupon he thrust his nose on to the end of my nose and, pushing hard, shouted with a deafening voice, "Nez – nez!" I haven't forgotten the French for nose to this day!

Upton House did get results and I am grateful to the school and staff for giving me a thirst for knowledge. Part of my schooling involved learning to type, which I mastered and which I have found useful throughout my life. I was never one for sport but I enjoyed the woodwork class. The master was austere, the cane and book were often used but fortunately I escaped his anger. I do remember him standing behind me when I was sawing a piece of wood and saying, "Bowers, hold the saw straight." How proud I was to take home a polished piece of woodwork, a small book stand.

It was at Upton House Central School where boys in my class told me about sex, which until then I was ignorant about; my parents regarded the subject as taboo and they never told me anything about this important aspect of life – but parents didn't then. There is no denying that the sexual taboos of an earlier age were a cause of much unhappiness and psychological ill-health. Fortunately, I weathered the storm of temptations, and my association with the Scouts and church helped me to get things into perspective and to regard sexual matters as normal feelings. Loyalty, fidelity, and trust I instinctively believed should not offend the values that I learned in Sunday School and church.

There were some nice walks near to our home. Springfield Park was a mile away and Hackney marshes, flat green land and meadows, ran alongside the river Lea, which once generated water mills standing on the banks. Dick Turpin had a hideout there in the eighteenth century. I recall the barges going up the river pulled by large carthorses. Woe betide anyone on the river bank who got on the wrong side of the rope fixed to the horses. Such folly was dangerous and one could easily be swept into the river. From time to time it overflowed its banks and covered the fields around. It was a sight to see. I was terrified of water, but it fascinated me and on many occasions I would go down to the lock and stand and stare at the swirling water.

Hackney has a long tradition of welcoming new arrivals; its proximity to the docks made it a convenient stopping place for world travellers, many arriving from countries where they had suffered persecution. Arnold Wesker, the playwright, who also went to Upton House Central School, came to live in Hackney with his parents, who were Russian Jews. Stamford Hill, close by, was teeming with Jews. They came from everywhere and, by 1788, they had established their own cemetery in Hackney. They worked as tailors, jewellers, furriers, and shopkeepers, and they opened restaurants following their own traditions and dietary laws. Even the diarist, Samuel Pepys, visited Hackney. He records in his diary: "With my wife only to take ayre; it being very warm and pleasant, to Bowe and Old Ford; and thence to Hackney". Hackney was famous for its playhouse: "Hackney Empire", one of the Borough's treasured possessions, which stood in Mare Street. Most of the big names in show-business performed there, Marie Lloyd, Charlie Chaplin and W. C. Fields, to name but a few. A popular Victorian Music Hall song sung at the Empire had the refrain, "With a ladder and some glasses, you could see to Hackney marshes, if it wasn't for the houses in between".

St John's Parish Church, designed by James Spiller and consecrated in 1797, was famous for its bells. I recall hearing the bells pealing at midnight on Christmas Eve, making the magic of Christmas real, especially when I thought of the pillowcases of us four children hanging over the chimney grate, that we hoped would be filled with toys on Christmas morning.

In the winter of 1934, the minister of the church, Reverend Dr W. J. Smart, began a work of redemption, prompted by Francis Thompson's poem, "The Kingdom of God".

> "Yea, in the night, my Soul, my daughter,
> Cry, – clinging Heaven by the hems;
> And lo, Christ walking on the water
> Not of Gennesareth, but Thames!"

Dr Smart, accompanied by our scoutmaster, Douglas James, whom we called "Skip", went on Saturday nights to the Thames embankment in a motor-cycle sidecar to carry out a rescue operation and bring back someone sleeping rough underneath the arches of Waterloo Bridge, and take them to Southwold Road Methodist Church where a hostel was made ready to accommodate twelve men. There they were clothed, fed, and cared for, and helped to find employment. At that time there were three thousand homeless people in London every night. Most of them were not Londoners; they were mainly from the provinces, some from Wales, Scotland, Ireland, and the colonies, who came to London to search for work and sadly with nowhere to live. Many slept at night on the Thames embankment, in theatre doorways, in Trafalgar Square or down the Mall, anywhere, sometimes under cover, and sometimes in the rain or snow. Each of them had a story of failure; they were "Down-and-outs", without hope and at the point of despair. I shall never forget one night seeing these men sitting in front of a blazing fire, telling their stories. Dr Smart wrote a book about them called: *Christ of the Thames Embankment*, which became a best seller.

I joined the Scouts, transferring from the Cubs, and this occupied most of my spare time. Each year in August we spent a fortnight in camp in Devonshire. One year our tents were pitched in a place of great beauty, on the brow of a hill overlooking Barnstaple Bay. Behind us, in the distance, stretched vast tracts of unexplored hinterland, dense forests and wide open moors, while near at hand were terracotta fields and green pasturage, interspersed with patches of yellow harvest, where the piled up sheaves of ripening corn grew crisp in the August sun. To our right lay the coast of Westward Ho!, Woollacombe and Mortehoe, and on a clear day we saw, far away, the Welsh mountains; to our left lay Clovelly, England's loveliest village, tumbling down the steep, rugged cliffs to the water's edge. Before us was the sea, the blue sea of the North Devon coast, stretching away from the purple heathered cliffs at our feet to meet the cloudless blue sky at the far horizon. And here, in this veritable paradise of God, where sweet-scented honeysuckle abounded in every hedgerow and superb weather gladdened our days, we listened to the voice of nature as she spoke to our forebears when the world was young, and where every common bush was aflame with the glory of God.

For the first fortnight, a party of Scouts were on one the hilltop, and Guides on another. Every morning we stood outside our tents for morning worship. These moments were moments with God on the mount, when I knew that he was near me in every leaf that rustled and in the morning breeze; and, invariably, some skylark singing on the wing conjoined our praise for the glory of created things, and at even, after watching the sun set over the western sea, with a shaft of sometimes saffron, sometimes silver, sometimes crimson coming across the shimmering waters to the foothills, we worshipped God. How I recalled those indescribable sunsets in the winter's fogs in London. How I remembered those groups of young Scouts on Devon hilltops watching the sun dip into the sea, bathing the quiet departing day in a mystic hush, and then the harvest moon, soft but splendid, captured our attention with awe and wonder. Those fortnight camps were memorable. We enjoyed playing games and wandering over the wide fields and wooded slopes, our eyes open to the loveliness and wonder of the world.

Chapter Two

Leaving School, Other Relatives

Just before I reached the age of fifteen I decided to leave school and start work. I wanted to become a lawyer and I was fortunate enough to obtain an appointment in a firm of solicitors named: Thompson and Mattingly, of Carey Street, near to Lincoln's Inn Fields. Thompson had died and Mattingly, a very doddery old man, far too fat, was brought to the office by his wife, who was years younger, in a chauffer-driven car. Most mornings he arrived at 10 o'clock with a large Havana cigar in his mouth. He shuffled into his swivel chair in his large and comfortable office and sat there until his wife came for him early in the afternoon. Norman Beanland, a young solicitor who joined the partnership, was a kind man and took me along to the London Law Courts and at once a new life was opened to me. It was fascinating to go inside the Law Courts and to see judges with their colourful gowns and grey wigs. It wasn't long before I thought that the profession of the law was among the noblest open to me. I went to the Law Courts as frequently as I was able and sat listening with rapt attention to interesting cases like the divorce proceedings of Gracie Fields, the famous singer from Rochdale, and the legal case that came about in consequence of the sinking of the submarine *Thetis*. I discovered quickly that one would have to be a good listener to become a lawyer, but I also realized what a great deal of preparation was put into advocacy before standing up in court to plead a case. Soon after I started work I became aware of the seamy side of life, particularly in regard to sexual misconduct in divorce proceedings and the explicit details given during the various cases in the law courts.

In the office there were two stenographers, one in her middle thirties, who had a shock of red hair, was full of fun and clever at taking down letters at speed and typing them up for signature. The other woman was married; she took me in hand and taught me the rules of book-keeping. Both ladies were kind and helpful to me.

My weekly wage was fifteen shillings, and I had to work on Saturday mornings. For lunch, I went to Lyon's, where there was a waitress service. The waitresses were called "Nippies", pert young women with starched aprons and caps and ready smiles, which epitomized the swift, cheerful service expected by customers of Lyon's Teashops and Corner Houses. From the 1930s until after the war they were a national institution. I often had Welsh rarebit or a poached egg on toast for sixpence! I frequently walked through Lincoln's Inn Fields and wondered if one day my name would be on a brass plate as a solicitor. I had a zest for living and getting on and after two years I left the firm I worked for and went to one of the largest firm of solicitors and barristers in London, called Slaughter and May. The office was extremely busy and in a couple of months I felt at home and was sure that the legal profession was to be my career.

My grandmother on my father's side frequently used the word "persevere" to encourage me, but I had a long way to go because I left school before obtaining my school certificate. You will remember that grandmother lived next door with my grandfather, William Henry Bowers. He was born on the 13th April 1863. He came to London at the age of nine and was brought up by his grandmother. He started work at the age of twelve, with little schooling, and was apprenticed to his Uncle whose name was Slade, a medical box turner. He worked in a small factory at The Oval, Hackney.

Occasionally he would bring home a sackful of imperfect pieces of wood off-cuts; I would enjoy using them for building blocks. My grandfather liked his drink and when he finished work he called at

"The Green-Gate", a public house opposite the factory. The story is told that one day he came home drunk and emptied a sackful of wood-cuts and sawdust over my grandmother's bed. She told him that unless he stopped drinking she would leave him, and after that warning he never went to the public house again. He came under the influence of the Salvation Army. I remember, one Sunday morning, the Salvation Army Band playing hymns outside his house. It was my first introduction to the Salvation Army, an organization that later in life I had reason to admire.

My grandmother was called Elizabeth Ann Bowers. She was born on the 31st March 1863 at Bethnal Green. Her maiden name was Hills. Her mother kept a confectionery shop and she met my grandfather there. Her mother was very strict and wished her to have nothing to do with my grandfather. However, she relented eventually and they were married on 20th July 1887 in the parish church of South Hackney.

My great-grandfather, also called William Henry Bowers, was born at Halstead in Essex in 1839. For years he worked as ploughman and in 1885 he came to London where he opened a greengrocer's shop in Chatsworth Road, which he managed for thirty years. During this time he became interested in Methodism and was introduced to a young Methodist minister named Thomas Jackson, who had taken over a theatre called The Theatre Royal in Glenarm Road, where he gathered together a band of people for worship on Sundays. Within twelve months he had plans in hand for the building of a new church in Blurton Road, Clapton, to be named Clapton Park Tabernacle. It was opened for worship in 1885 at a cost of £3,000. The people had worked hard to raise the money, in spite of the fact that there was extreme poverty and widespread unemployment; wages for those who had employment was extremely low. Children lacked sufficient food and clothing and so the minister instituted free breakfasts for them and he also opened a medical dispensary and set up a clothes store. A Legal Aid Bureau was available for those who needed advice on legal matters.

Great-grandfather Bowers attended this church for the rest of his life and played an active part in its ministry. He conducted open-air services on summer evenings, at which my aunt Lilly played the harmonium. I'm told that he stood on a soap box and attracted people by banging a bucket with a stick He told the small audience about the unsearchable riches of Christ. He was blessed with a powerful voice and when singing in church he was often heard to shout out "Amen" during the sermon. He died aged 84 in 1923, the year of my birth.

My great-grandmother was born in 1843 at Braintreein Essex. Her maiden name was Slade, and she had the biblical name of Hannah. She served in the family greengrocer's shop for many years. On Sundays she went to the Salvation Army. She always wore the uniform and was a devout worshipper.

My mother's name was Mogg. Her father was Samuel Mogg, born in Plymouth in 1854. For years he served in the Royal Navy and was away from home for months at a time. He was jovial, short in build, with deep brown eyes and black curly hair. After serving in the navy he became a boiler engineer and was an expert in installing boilers. He died at the age of 82 after a series of strokes. I remembered visiting him hospital and couldn't understand what he meant when he said to me, "Bubbles" – his nickname for me – "There's a battleship under the bed." He was a loveable man.

My grandmother Mogg was born in Bethnal Green. Her maiden name was Haakon. She had nine children: Samuel, who was killed in August 1917 in a battle in France during the First World War, Maud, who sadly died from a heart attack on the eve of her wedding, and there was Dorothy, my mother, and her three brothers, William, Thomas, and Percy, whom I knew well. The other children were stillborn.

Grandmother Mogg was a strong character. Her house in Bonner Road was next door to where Bishop Bonner once lived. It was always open house. Christmas Day for many years was spent at Grandma Mogg's house. They were happy occasions, especially the roast turkey with all the trimmings and the pudding sprinkled with brandy and lit, its flames reaching up to the ceiling. I remember sitting before a large log fire in the parlour, the family gathered around and being enthralled by my grandmother's stories.

Her living room was full of fascinating objects. I remember the large parrot's cage and the parrot with its green and red feathers and frightening black beak, which one day nipped my brother's finger as he stuck it through the bars while feeding the bird. In the corner were two enormous white ivory tusks, which my grandfather brought home from overseas. On the sideboard was a large ship's compass. I wondered if he was related to another William Mogg, who sailed the high seas and whose diaries were kept at Southampton University.

I felt a sense of awe in the presence of my grandmother. Sadly, her house was destroyed in the raids on London in 1941; she was badly injured and died as a result of those injuries. She truly believed she was a descendant of the King of Norway.

Christmas 1938 was the last time we spent together as a family in our home. By then the clouds of war were gathering and father was regularly working overtime in the War Office.

An elderly friend of father's came to us on Christmas Day. His name was Knight, and we used to say that he was Knight by name and Knight by nature! In the First World War he stood on Waterloo Station dressed in an army great coat that stretched to his ankles. He shouted out to the troops as they came off the train: "This is the way to the underground". "You'll soon be there, mate", came the jocular reply from a soldier. He took it in the right spirit and worked tirelessly for troops as they returned bedraggled and battle weary from France. For this service he was awarded the MBE. We always looked forward to his visits because he brought us a variety of sweets such as sugar pigs and other goodies. How we loved them.

I particularly liked him to talk of his life and adventures and on this Christmas Day as we sat round the fire he told us his favourite text in the New Testament, stood up and recited it in his clear, strong voice: "Eye hath not seen, nor ear heard, neither have entered into the heart of man, the things which God hath prepared for them that love him". (1. COR. 2:9, AV). As I looked out of our parlour window and saw people passing by, I turned to Mr Knight and said: "I dare you to go to the front door and shout out this verse at the top of your voice." I didn't expect him to take up the challenge. However, to my astonishment he went to the front door and shouted it out at the top of his voice. I have never forgotten his witness or the verse of scripture. He was a dear man and we loved him and looked forward to his visits – not just for the sweets, I must add.

In the summer of 1939 we spent our holiday at Clacton-on-Sea and it was a joy to be driven in a large limousine car by a friend of father's. We stayed at a boarding house near the sea front. On the wall of the lounge was a framed text: "Don't worry, it may never happen". But it did happen; our holiday was cut short as father was recalled to the War Office. It seemed that war with Germany was inevitable. Preparations by the Civil Defence were taking place all over London, and sandbags were being filled and placed outside important buildings in Hackney. I remember going with some of the older Scouts to Hackney Town Hall to pack gas masks carefully into cardboard boxes, which in due course were to be issued to every man, woman, and child. As I left the town hall I saw Sir Oswald Mosley standing on the roof of a London taxi and addressing a huge crowd of men, most of whom wore black shirts. The police were there in force and some were on horseback. I felt a sense of fear go through me, and I ran home as quickly as I could.

As I walked through Lincoln's Inn Field one lunch hour I saw men digging trenches in the well laid out lawns. There was an air of expectancy; gas masks were being distributed to every household, and everyone thought that war with Germany was to be announced at any time, except the Prime Minister, Mr Neville Chamberlain.

Four days before Christmas, £20 million was allocated to provide 10 million steel shelters known as "Anderson shelters", which were erected at the end of gardens and, in some houses, in downstairs rooms. Air raid sirens were tested in London and the big cities, and for the first time we heard the mournful wailing of the sirens that was to become so familiar. The "all clear" brought a sense of relief that we could, at least for a time, get on with our lives. It seemed that the Cold War had begun, but life went on much the same as usual.

As a family we never wanted for anything. I do know that on Sunday afternoons when we came back from Sunday School, the table was loaded with sandwiches and luscious cakes, Victoria jam sponge and chocolate cream, which mother baked so excellently, but

Left to right: Allan, Mother, Grace, and Hilda

she said, "If war breaks out we shan't be sitting down to teas like
this again." And I thought that father would have to cut down on
smoking Craven A.

Christmas 1938 was a white Christmas, a rare occurrence in
London. December had started unusually mild, but by the middle of
the month it became bitterly cold, with gales in the channel disrupt-
ing ferries, followed by a brief thaw and hard frosts again on the day
before Christmas. On Christmas Day there were four inches of snow
in Trafalgar Square and winter sports were possible on Hampstead
Heath. The roads were white and deserted. In the evening of Boxing
Day I recalled going to the front door with mother to put out the milk
bottles for the delivery the next morning. Ice-cold air blew in our
faces as we opened the door, and we felt happy and contented to
return to the warmth of the sitting room with the blazing open fire.
Somehow it all seemed safe and enduring, and yet there were
thoughts of an unexpected future in our minds. It was still peace but
no one really trusted it. Indeed it was the hush before the storm. I
have to admit the name Adolph Hitler was virtually unknown to me

at the time, but soon it became part of the headlines of the daily newspapers and his treatment of the Jews in Germany and his lust for power became regular items of news. Neville Chamberlain followed a policy of appeasement. In September 1938 he signed the Munich agreement, approving the transfer of German-speaking border areas of Czechoslovakia to Germany. He claimed that the agreement was "symbolic" of the desire of their two peoples never to go to war with one another again. Fear of an immediate world war was followed by universal relief, and an almost hysterical acclamation for Neville Chamberlain. I shall never forget the picture of him waving a piece of paper signed by Hitler. However, this was soon followed by disenchantment with the Munich agreement.

Chapter Three

War, London Bombing

War was declared by Britain on Sunday 3rd September 1939; I had just turned sixteen. The declaration took place after German troops occupied the Czech capital of Prague and invaded Poland. I remember that fateful Sunday very well indeed. I went to church as usual but the service conducted by our minister, Reverend Dr W. J. Smart, was brought to a speedy end when he told the congregation that we would be at war with Germany from 11 o'clock. I heard from father how Zeppelin airships from Germany had dropped bombs over London in the First World War. I wondered if, with all Hitler's modern bombers, we would be bombed within hours of the declaration. I hurried home to see my mother standing on the steps of our house holding a gas mask. She had tears in her eyes and our next-door neighbour, an air raid warden, had fainted, being so overcome with the news. I confess that though I was frightened I felt a sense of exhilaration, but I was not old enough to realize the full implication of what war meant.

The months passed by and life went on much as usual; there was the occasional air raid siren but no enemy action. I think we were all lulled into thinking that nothing would happen. In the summer of 1940 I went to stay with my brother, Stanley, who was a pastor in the Kingsbridge Methodist Circuit, and who lived in the charming village of Chillington, near Slapton Sands. During the holiday I spent happy hours riding pillion on my brother's motor-cycle as he visited members of his churches scattered over the countryside. As the Cold War went on the thought of any enemy action was far from our thoughts. However, one bright sunny afternoon we saw a plane high in the sky above Salcombe, the little seaport in Devon's pretty south, with its wonderful views over land and water and its narrow streets beside the estuary. Suddenly the plane swooped down and released a stick of bombs. We watched it happen with incredulity. There were no Royal Air Force planes to intercept this lone bomber, which disappeared on the horizon leaving a trail of smoke in the sky.

Our curiosity was heightened as to where the bombs had fallen, so we went in search and found an enormous crater large enough to hold two London buses. I climbed down into the crater and found a jagged piece of metal as a souvenir to take home.

I fell in love with Chillington and spent some time looking at the blacksmith's forge, where farmers brought their horses for shoeing. The surrounding green fields and lanes were such a contrast to the busy city of London where I worked and to which I was to return all too soon. One day we met Donald Robinson, a friend of Stanley's and a Methodist minister, as we walked along the beach. He gave me a little book to read, entitled, *What is a Living Church?*, which was to influence my life, though at the time I had no clear idea as to what my future would be.

On the Sunday afternoon of my holiday I went to the Methodist church in the centre of the village. The preacher was an ex-naval chaplain and he began the service by saying, "Let the Gospel bells ring." The small congregation sang lustily and I enjoyed the service. Rural Methodism attracted me and the Devonshire people made me feel so welcome.

When I returned home life seemed to go on much the same. I enjoyed working at Slaughter and May and I began to think how I might begin studies for becoming a lawyer; the thought was growing upon me that lawyers were indispensable to any civilized society. I also felt a strong urge to improve my painting. My first love was oils, and I enjoyed copying the "Red Boy" which I gave to a young lady in the church, the thought being that this might stir up her interest in me. I also copied a painting of Lord Baden Powell, the Chief Scout. His book *Scouting for Boys* gripped my imagination and deepened my interest in scouting, as did our Sunday church parades. I attended morning and evening worship and afternoon Sunday School. These weekly activities kept us occupied and made the war seem far away. However, things were not going well in the political field. Germany was preparing for a long war and the newspapers were making headline news of all that Hitler was doing. By August barrage balloons, a defence against low flying aircraft, could be seen in the sky over London, and after dark the sky was a network of searchlights. Since we did not have an Anderson shelter I helped father clear out a corner of the cellar and make it comfortable, because he was sure that we would all be safe there. As I remember it, the summer was very hot and the days seemed long. Only the barrage balloons and the searchlights at night were a reminder that all was not well and that the storm was about to break out after the hush, and break it did.

It began on a Saturday afternoon in early September. I had just finished dinner and was sitting on the patio with Grace and mother when the sirens sounded. I looked up, and to my astonishment I saw high in the sky and flying in formation what appeared to be enemy aircraft. They looked like a flight of silver birds in the sunshine, but soon we saw RAF Spitfires, moving among them and splitting up the squadrons. It was high drama and hard to believe that such an engagement was taking place. Mother, my sister and I rushed into the cellar shelter and stayed for over two hours until we heard the all clear siren. When we went into the garden we could see smoke on the horizon coming from the East India Docks, a prime target for the German planes. When father returned from the War Office that night he said there were fires still burning, and as darkness fell we could see that the sky was red. Later that night the bombers were back, the battle of Britain had begun, and East London was heavily bombed until the dawn. I found it hard to believe that this was happening. My mother sat in corner of our cellar shelter sitting inside the large bath that we always used on Friday nights. On my way to work on

Monday morning I saw that fire engines were still operating, damping down fires, and in places there were houses reduced to rubble. Each night we spent in our shelter and I had that feeling that by daylight our house would be bombed. It was a horrible experience and I wondered how it was all going to end. Would our family life, which seemed so secure, become a casualty of the war?

Hearing of the dreadful bombing of London, my brother telephoned father at the War Office in London and urged him to close the house as soon as possible. The plan was that I should leave Slaughter and May and with mother and Grace go to Chillington until the bombing of London ceased. Father would stay at the War Office, where there were deep shelters, and we would leave for Devon within a day or two. And so, early on the morning of the 14th of September, Grace and I said goodbye to mother and father. I had a strange feeling of foreboding and was reluctant to leave the family home. My last word to mother was to urge her to join us within a day or two. That previous night there had been heavy bombing and many people were killed. On the journey to Paddington station there was evidence everywhere of houses down and fire engines at work. The journey to Devonshire was uneventful and when we arrived at Kingsbridge we felt safe after the terrible ordeal of the past week, but anxious for our parents who, with other hundreds of families, would experience raids with increasing intensity. What was happening in London was also happening in many of the cities throughout the country. Fortunately, thousands of children had been evacuated from danger zones into the relative safety of the countryside.

It was a great relief for Grace and me to stay with Stanley, who had digs with a kind lady, her husband and daughter. It was so peaceful and free from the sirens, but we simply longed for mother to join us and when we heard the wireless news we listened with increased intensity, hoping and praying that the bombing would soon end. It did not and for the next few nights the bombing of London grew even worse. A large number of air battles took place, but the RAF gave measure for measure and hundreds of enemy planes were shot down or brought down by anti-aircraft fire.

On the 23rd of September, just as we were going down to breakfast, a letter was pushed under our bedroom door. It was from grandma Mogg and in her shaking handwriting she informed us that on the 19th September our house had sustained a direct hit and mother had been killed. Father had been rescued from the rubble and had been admitted to Homerton Hospital. Grandma finished her letter saying, "Come home as quickly as possible." Stanley and I left Chillington after breakfast and caught the first train to Paddington. The journey took several hours and it was nightfall before we reached Paddington and already the sirens had sounded. Everywhere was blacked out and with some difficulty we caught a bus to Bethnal Green and walked along the dark streets to 37 Bonner Road. When we entered the house, not a word was spoken for a while, and then Grandma pointed to the mantelpiece on which there were several tomatoes and the clock turned on its side. "Your mother," she said, "came to see me a few days ago and brought those tomatoes, and because the clock wouldn't work she turned it on its side. I can't bring myself to touch them now that she has gone." An oil lamp, burning faintly, shed a light over the table and I thought for a moment of those happy Christmas dinners, when the family was gathered round the table and the roast turkey was set ready for carving. I simply could not bring myself to believe that mother, whom I said goodbye to only a few days ago, was dead!

That night we were accommodated in the Victoria Park Hospital, only a stone's throw from grandmother's house. Uncle Tom, one of her sons, was fire watching on the roof of the hospital. He was a brave man and risked his life to save five nurses in a section of the hospital that had been bombed. For this act of bravery he was awarded a special medal.

Sleeping that night was almost impossible, for we were in the basement and many of the patients suffering from tuberculosis had been transferred to a makeshift ward in the basement and their constant coughing was disturbing.

The next morning we went to Hommerton General Hospital, where father was recovering from the terrible ordeal he had been through. He had no recollection of the actual bombing. That fateful night they had decided to stay under the stairs, where they thought it would be safe. Apparently the bomb went through the house and the blast brought down several houses, killing mother and fourteen other people, including four small children. Miraculously, two beams fell on either side of father and he was protected from falling masonry and rubble. He was not injured, but badly shocked. Pastor James Kirby our local pastor, an ambulance driver, helped rescue father and take him from the ruins to hospital. My grandfather's house next door was standing, and fortunately it was possible to bore a hole through the cellar wall to rescue father, but sadly mother was found dead.

After visiting father we made our way to 81 Elderfield Road to see our house, which was a heap of rubble. We were devastated but we were not alone; large centres of population suffered heavily the night mother died. All the London Boroughs showed long casualty lists. Deaths occurred in offices, factories, schools, public vehicles, air raid shelters, and in the open country. The thousands of deaths included members of the peerage. Sometimes whole families were wiped out. The names of individuals meant little save to those who knew and loved them and mourned their loss. It was fitting that these names were enrolled in the Westminster Abbey Book of Remembrance, kept at the heart of the Commonwealth and among the most illustrious of the nation's dead in commemoration of their suffering and a tribute to their sacrifice.

Father was unable to attend the funeral of mother. She was only forty-two, and loved her family deeply. The loss of mother completely devasted father, and it was weeks of careful nursing in the home of Mrs Short, where my brother was living, that enabled him to make a full recovery. I was fortunate to join a firm of solicitors in Kingsbridge, and to get on with my life, though I knew that things would never be the same again for any of us and especially for father, who dearly loved mother. Her death had a profound affect upon me and worshipping in the Methodist church in Chillington set me thinking more deeply about the meaning of my life, but I found it difficult to reconcile my belief in a personal, caring God with all the suffering that was going on in the world as a result of war. Yet, I felt the pull of the Church, and somehow felt I could put things together and survive the ordeals that had come my way. I never ceased thanking God for my brother, who played a vital part in ensuring the safety of Grace and me. We were a united family and the tragedy had the effect of forming us into a strong, caring unity. Since mother had us all within four years, we were able to enjoy each other's company, to see each other's interests and to squabble as children sometimes do, but mainly to have a happy relationship which has lasted throughout our lives.

My brother Stanley entered the Methodist ministry and after twenty years transferred to the Anglican church where he had a fulfilling ministry for over twenty years at St Michael The Archangel, Two Mile Hill, Bristol. He obtained a Bachelor of Divinity degree with honours at London University.

Grace, my younger sister, went to train as a nurse at King's College Hospital, London, where she qualified as a State Registered Nurse and State Midwife. My elder sister, Hilda, who obtained her Master of Arts degree at Bedford College, went on to the Sorbonne in Paris, where she completed a course of research studies, presenting in French a thesis on the religious philosophy of Benjamin Constant (1767–1830) and was awarded a degree of Doctorat de L'Universite de Paris with the mention "très honorable".

It could truly be said that we were an ecumenical family, my brother an Anglican priest, my elder sister, Hilda, a Roman Catholic, and my younger sister, Grace, an Anglican. I remained a Methodist, and though we were members of different denominations we always enjoyed a happy relationship and worshipped from time to time in each other's churches. And despite the trauma of mother's tragic death we remained committed Christians.

After some months in Chillington I went to stay with my godmother in Bournemouth. My aunt and uncle were Congregationalists. They were devout Christians and I learned much from their example and loving care. Once again I was able to join a firm of solicitors in Southbourne. It seemed as though God was setting me up to train in law. The head of the firm, a Mr Richards, was a charming gentleman who took an interest in me, and I met him at the Southbourne Methodist Church where he and his wife worshipped.

Chapter Four

Life from a New Angle

In the hymn by William Cowper, it is said that God moves in a mysterious way, his wonders to perform. It seemed providential that I went to Bournemouth to be with my godmother, and I am sure that this move was a turning point in my life. My aunt showed me all the love of a mother and we became very close. She and my uncle, by their godly living, showed me the likeness of Christ, and their lovely home looking over the river Stour, near to Tuckton Bridge, was a haven of rest. Fortunately, Southbourne Methodist Church was nearby and I was introduced to a warm fellowship where there was a strong Bible class and a lot of young people of my own age group. I read again and again the little book, *What is a Living Church?* given to me by Donald Robinson, which offered me fresh insight into the witness of Jesus and the impact that he made upon his disciples and how they became witnesses. It gave me a new focus on faith and set me thinking more deeply upon the meaning of faith.

In the spring of 1941, while walking along Fisherman's Walk, a delightful, wooded part of Bournemouth, I saw a large number of young men being drilled by a Flight Sergeant. They had bronzed faces, looked a picture of health and even seemed to be enjoying the drill. I knew that soon I would receive my call-up papers and then I noticed a large recruiting poster that read: "See life from a new angle

– join the Royal Air Force". Two things occurred to me: "Fisherman's Walk" and "See life from a new angle". Did not Jesus, when walking along the sea shore of Galilee, call the fishermen to follow him, and when they discovered Jesus, did not they see life from a new angle? This event became a turning point in my life, for in joining the Royal Air Force that summer I saw life from a new angle.

I began my life in the Royal Air Force at Cardington and, after initial training, was posted to Battersea Park Polytechnic to train as a wireless operator, air crew. I was billeted with an elderly Welsh couple who looked after me with great care and treated me like a son. I began to think even more deeply about God's providence and I couldn't get out of my mind the thought that there was divine purpose at work in the world and that I and every other human being was part of that purpose, so I felt safe and secure. I believed I had the Fatherly care of God. While at Battersea I decided I didn't wish

Royal Air Force, 1946

to become a wireless operator, air crew, because that would inevitably involve going on bombing raids and, though I was part of the war machine, I couldn't bring myself to be involved in air raids that were aimed at destruction. I had always a high regard for the medical profession and so I transferred to the medical branch and was sent on an anatomy and physiology course at Sidmouth in Devon.

Before leaving Battersea I went to see my minister to enquire about training as a Local Preacher in the Methodist Church. He gave me what in Methodism is called "a note to preach". When I arrived at Sidmouth I was billeted in The Royal Glen Hotel, which was grand indeed. I attended the Sidmouth Methodist Church and one Sunday I was invited to conduct a morning service. I made a note in my diary, Sunday 29th November 1942, and I preached on the text from Hebrews 13, verse 8: "Jesus Christ is the same yesterday and today and for ever". On Sunday evenings a group of young men serving in the Royal Air Force were invited to a fellowship meeting in a room over the bakery that was opposite the church. I shall always remember those evenings when we read the Bible together and studied it, after which we had freshly baked rolls with butter, and strawberry jam, a rare treat in those austere days. The sea front was covered with barbed wire and Connaught Gardens, once a showpiece of Sidmouth, was looking drab. Machine-gun posts had been erected in concrete bunkers, and the large hotels on the sea front were filled with RAF personnel. Exeter, the noble city of the West, had come under heavy bombing in the devastating raids of May 1942, when several churches were damaged or destroyed and the cathedral suffered heavy damage on the south side of the choir. I visited the cathedral and in one corner I saw the visitors' book. The last entry read: "So long thy power hath blessed me, sure it still will lead me on" (70 years). The handwriting was shaky but it made me think that this was the testimony of one who, like the author, John Henry Newman, had proved the staying power of God in difficult times.

When I finished the course at Sidmouth I was posted to Royal Air Force hospital at St Athens, for practical training in the wards and in the operating theatre. The operating side of the course fascinated me.

Once there was a plane returning from Casablanca that crashed, and some of the survivors were brought to the hospital. Through the night a team of doctors and nurses worked on the casualties in the operating theatre and I, a trainee medical orderly, assisted a nurse in the surgical ward. It was as if I had been plunged in at the deep end in this aspect of training, but it gave me a great admiration for the surgeons, the nurses and their care for their patients.

Upon completing my course I was posted to a unit of the Air Ministry in Ruislip, on the outskirts of London, to spend the remainder of my years in the Royal Air Force engaged in medical statistics. It was there that I met Kenneth MacKenzie, an RAF chaplain, who helped me in my Local Preachers' studies. On Sundays, when I was off duty, I went to Westminster Central Hall to hear the Reverend Dr Edwin Sangster preach to a vast congregation. I read in a daily newspaper that there was no preacher in Britain at that time who could draw such large crowds with the magic of his words and the magnetism of his personality. I so loved his preaching that I went to the Central Hall at every opportunity and it was under Dr Sangster's ministry that I learned some important things in the art of preaching. I read his books, and one which influenced me was *The Path to Perfection* 1943, Epworth Press, in which he made a valuable contribution to the idea of holiness for which he was awarded the degree of Doctor of Philosophy of London University. The preface to the book revealed a man of intense spirituality and holiness and was of unusual interest to me with my experience of bombing in London when I read:

This book has been written during the period in which I forsook my home to share the life of bombed-out people in a public air-raid shelter, that is not intended as a covert apology for any deficiencies in the book. It is hoped that the work will stand without that. It is stated merely for the slight interest it may have for a social student of the future who will wonder how people spent their time underground. When the last incendiary had been put out and the last group of homeless people received and made welcome, I filled the house of the vigil which still had to be kept by thinking on perfection. If that seemed a little mad to some who read this, I can only reply it was the way in which I kept sane.

Sangster, The Path to Perfection

I mention this dedicated man of God because it was this kind of preaching that I needed at that time. In his presence and by his preaching I felt the spirit of Christ reaching out to me. He enabled me to get closer to the fuller intensity, drama, and daily practice of the presence of Christ, which was far from easy in the early days of the war days serving in the Royal Air Force. It would not be an exaggeration to say that he was a jewel of the church. Serving in the RAF and living a communal life in a barrack room with twenty-eight men from different walks of life was a testing experience. As I look back on my five and a half years' service I know that I was pulled in two ways, one towards what might be called the primacy of pleasure, the other the primacy of character. The pleasure principle expressed itself in the catch-phrases of the day: "Have a good time", and "I couldn't care less". In a mixed camp where young men and women were working together the temptation for sexual relationships was very strong. Widespread drinking or "pub crawling" as it was called, frequently took place on pay days, though since I never felt the temptation to join in those outings I never knew what it was like to be drunk as some were when they came back to barracks.

The primacy of character was a strong pull and I knew that I owed so much to my parents for the upbringing they had given me and also to the church to which I belonged. It was in the early days of being in the RAF that I gave a great deal of thought to things in life which had to do with values. My first concern with questions about the Christian faith and theology in actual life came with my contact with the men in the barrack room. For the first time in my life I was faced with a double crisis: the crisis of relevance and the crisis of identity. I asked myself time and time again two questions: "How could Jesus Christ who lived two thousand years ago be relevant to my situation?", and, the greater of the two questions: "Who am I?" My service number was 1451813 and I wore a tag around my neck for identity purposes, but deep down I knew that I was more than a number and somehow I knew that it was only a religious outlook that would help me deal with the question of my true identity.

Christianity first lodged in my mind when, in the barrack room, I made friends with a convinced atheist. Talking with him had the effect of making me examine carefully the reasons I had for believing in God. I could literally say, "Thank God for the atheist", for had he not been there I would probably not have questioned my faith and it was this questioning that made me search for a meaning and to find understanding through faith. Being without my mother and having no home to go to I was thrown back on the fellowship of the church. Westminster Central Hall on Sunday mornings, with Dr Sangster to listen to, and my visit across London to my childhood church on Sunday afternoons, provided me with an anchor. Christianity came seeping through me and I knew that Christ's powerful presence was something I was beginning to feel more than ever. I thought even more seriously about the challenge of Christ in the gospels and the cost of discipleship. I thought of Jesus as a man who belonged intensely to this world, which he came to redeem; a man who was part of life, knowing its joys and sorrows, but who rose above life's demands, displaying a peace and poise beyond understanding. I discovered him to be unique because, although he completely identified with life, he was sharply different from it. He held thoughts so different from others; he brought down to earth the rules by which we may all live together in peace and harmony.

I had been received into the membership of the Methodist Church at the age of fourteen, but there hadn't been a radical change in my life. Membership, or confirmation as it is now called, left little change in my way of thinking and acting. I continued going to church because it was the wish of my parents, but it was more out of habit than a deep desire. However, as I described in Chapter 1, the church organist befriended me, and introduced me to religious philosophy during our long walks when we talked about the values of beauty, truth and goodness and the sheer joy of living and loving and knowing the world around us. Undoubtedly his friendship laid the foundation upon which I built and in due course gave me an encounter with the living Christ. This encounter occurred towards the end of March 1942 when, alone in the Medical Statistical Office where I worked, I felt a sense of the presence of Christ as never before. Could it be called a direct sense of communion with the Divine brought about by prayer? I believe it was just this, but it was real and from that day onward life was different. It was life from a new angle. I made an entry in my diary at the time; the date was 23rd March, 1942. It read, "I gave my life to Christ".

I had already started training as a Local Preacher in the Methodist Church, and my studies took up most of my off-duty time. I recall the first sermon I preached in a small Methodist church in East London. There were six people in the congregation. The text was: "Come unto me all you are heavy laden and I will give you rest". It seems hard to believe that fifty-six years later on the site of that small Methodist Church stands the Kingsway International Centre, the spiritual home for 5,000 worshippers. God truly moves in mysterious way his wonders to perform.

After completing my training as a Local Preacher and being commissioned to preach while still in the RAF, I felt that God was calling me to become a minister of the Methodist Church. I was twenty-two. I had little knowledge of the Bible and I knew that there would be a long period of study if I were to pass the entrance examinations for the ministry.

Christianity has rightly been described as "the religion of the cross". Jesus spoke about taking up the cross daily. It was at the cross where I first started my study of the Gospels and that took me to the centre of Christ's suffering. And whatever small sacrifice I made, whatever denial of self in those long weary days of the war, it was taking a continual look at the "crucified one" that enabled me to prepare for the examinations and, before the war ended, to be accepted as a candidate for the ministry of the Methodist Church.

A candidate for the Methodist Ministry at the end of the war was unable to proceed to theological college for training because the colleges hadn't reopened, and so I was appointed by the Methodist Conference to go to Matlock in Derbyshire as a pre-collegiate probationer. I was given an early release from the RAF and, in September 1946, took a train to Matlock. I was wearing my "demob suit" and had with me two sermons, but I was sure that God was with me on this new part of my journey of faith. I sat next to a middle-aged man and discovered that he was a Local Preacher in the Matlock Trinity Circuit to which I had been appointed. He was to greatly influence my life in the future months. When I arrived at Matlock station he gave me directions to get to the Superintendent's manse. I shall not forget George Poyser. He not only taught me to drive a car but, more importantly, he taught me that in loving Jesus everything else would fall into place. How true that was.

Chapter Five

Derbyshire

Walter James Morgan, a Welshman, was the Superintendent Minister, a kind man. At our first meeting he gave me a bust of John Wesley that I've treasured ever since. Sadly, soon after I arrived in the circuit, he had a heart attack and died. I had to take over the responsibilities of a Superintendent Minister and to care for eight churches, my main church being at Cromford, the village that Allison Uttley, the writer of children's books, described as "A misty, blue village of stone amongst the rocks and hills". It may have been a village of stone, but the people had hearts of gold and took me into their homes and offered me their generous hospitality.

This widespread rural circuit took me through some of the most lovely Derbyshire countryside. I bought a BSA 250 cc motor-cycle, the cheapest method of travel, as I had very little money to spare in those days. Could there be a more enjoyable experience on a sunny day than driving over hill and dale to the small chapels in the Derbyshire villages for which I had pastoral care? In a quaint village called Wensley I became friendly with a man called Norman Taylor, who was a teacher at Woodhouse Grove school. He was a Local Preacher in the circuit. I could rightly call him a "Barnabas" because he was a great encourager and helped me to face up to the challenge of caring for the churches. At that time there was much talk at the

Matlock 1946 (first appointment)

Methodist Conference of reconstructing, and more than once Norman exclaimed, "It's not a matter of reconstructing, it's a question of rebirth." He felt strongly that there was a great blindness among many of the Church leaders, and that at the local level the people were so occupied with raising money and getting the administration right that they didn't have time to look at Jesus, the head of the church, militant and triumphant! I remember how strongly Norman felt about the need for revival throughout Methodism, and I recall him saying, "So we dither; we need the fire of the early Methodists, we need their zeal and commitment." It was the great faith of Norman that inspired me at the beginning of my ministry.

Another such person was Muriel Willmott, who was the secretary of Willersley Castle, a Methodist Guild Holiday Home situated at Cromford, the former home of Sir Richard Arkwright, a 200-year-old listed building occupying a magnificent position on the edge of the Peak District overlooking the River Derwent. Muriel, a delightful Christian, persuaded the local Director to allow me to live in the Home Farm building, called Derwent House, at the bottom of the drive that led to the castle. It was in an idyllic position. From my bedroom window on the second floor I could see over the meadow the River Derwent and the great rocks known as "Scarthin Nick". The parish church of Cromford, where Sir Richard Arkwright used to worship, was nestling close to the river. I couldn't believe my good fortune in being housed in such a pleasant situation.

Muriel was a gifted lady; she had the ability to make the guests roar with laughter at her comical singing and come to a quiet hush when she spoke about Jesus Christ. We talked much about the power of Jesus and she spoke to me out of the richness of her spiritual storehouse. She was like a sturdy tree whose fruit was ripe and ready to fall. Her faith and energy not only impressed me, they enabled me to catch her enthusiasm and to pursue my task with zeal. She coined the phrase, "Victorious Living".

In September 1947 a new assistant secretary was appointed, a young lady named Betty Bird. She had blue eyes and auburn hair and was most attractive. I was delighted when I knew that she would be working alongside Muriel Willmott. She had responsibility for leading walks and preparing evening entertainment for the guests. Her home was in the small village of Weston-on-Trent, about seven miles from the city of Derby. She was born into a Methodist family, her parents being pillars of the Methodist church in the village, which had one Post Office that was also a shop and there was a Co-operative shop as well. Her parents, Ethel and Harry Bird had three children: Harry, her elder brother, Betty, and John, her younger brother. Her parents were farmers and ran a mixed farm that was largely arable and milking. Her father had a splendid herd of cows and until automatic milking was introduced each cow had to be milked by hand. I recall seeing them in the sheds, each cow having a name, Honeybell, Bluebell, Dorothy, to name but a few; they all looked alike when they were grazing in the fields but Betty's father knew each one by name.

Methodist preachers had reason to be grateful to Betty's parents, for they could be sure of warm hospitality at the farm after preaching on Sundays. During the war years when it was difficult to get eggs and butter they helped visiting preachers by giving them such things before they returned home. The farmhouse was large, a beautiful old house with two staircases, four bedrooms and an attic where the maids had their bedroom. Downstairs was the lounge, dining room, kitchen, dairy, and extended larder and milking parlour. There was a stone-flagged hall at the end of which was a tall grandfather clock in a beautiful oak case. Etched on the glass face was the text: "God is love", which always held my attention when visiting Betty's home. The large window at the back of the house overlooked fields that stretched down to the River Trent, creating a very pleasant view.

The farmhouse kitchen contained bronze pans, which in the winter were used to warm the beds. Betty's mother was a good cook and a variety of appetizing smells would come from the kitchen, especially the smell of newly baked bread. The dairy was used for cream and butter making and at various times of the year there were hams hanging from the ceiling and sides of bacon hanging on the wall. All the water came from a deep well, and had to be drawn from a pump in the yard.

Betty went to the small village school and, when she was ten, to The High School for Girls in Derby. The motto of the school was: "The fear of the Lord is the beginning of wisdom". She was a pupil there from 1931 to1938, worked hard, and obtained the General School Examination Certificate of London University, reaching a credit standard in English, Geography, Religious Knowledge, and French. After her schooling she trained as a shorthand-typist and held a number of important posts in Derby and Belper during the war years. Our friendship developed and we became strongly attached to each other. There was much to be happy about in this because we had interests in common and shared our love of Christ and his church.

I shall never forget the winter of 1947 because there was a fall of snow which stayed over the countryside for a number of weeks. It seemed like a kind of magic that made the meadows, trees and the great rocks look beautiful in their whiteness.

Christmas Day at the castle was always one to be remembered. The staff greeted the guests before breakfast singing: "Christians, awake, salute the happy morn". A large Christmas tree stood at the bottom of the wide staircase in the hall of the castle. The roads seemed quiet, with no traffic. The hills and valleys were white with snow. Holly and ivy decorated the hall and everyone was warm, happy and jolly, and the food was plentiful. I managed to get to my preaching appointments without falling off my motorbike. Truly 1947 was one of the happiest years of my life. Willersley Castle and the fellowship I had with the guests was helpful to me in my work.

I had the special privilege of ministering to the staff. Before breakfast every morning there was a "Quiet Time" for closer union with Christ, meditation, and prayer. Betty used to lead some of the Quiet Times and they were a real blessing. Sunday evenings were always special. After the evening meal a sacred concert was held with hymn singing and various performances by the staff and guests. Betty and I discovered all the nooks and crannies of the splendid old building and "Lover's Walk" in the extensive grounds along by the River Derwent, which led to Matlock Bath, so beautiful that it was sometimes referred to as the "Switzerland of England", a mecca for many visitors to the Peak District. How privileged I was to be living in the spacious and delightful grounds of Willersley Castle. Many people will be indebted to the group of businessmen who, in 1927, with strong faith and vision, purchased Willersley Castle as a Methodist Guild Holiday Centre and opened it on Friday 25th May, 1928.

During the Second World War it was taken over by the Ministry of Health and used as a maternity hospital. In a report in the *Daily Telegraph* a reporter who visited the castle wrote: "Surely nowhere in all England could such a gracious house in such glorious surroundings have been chosen for those London women whose babies might otherwise have been born under perilous conditions." Over 4,000 babies were born in the castle during the war years, at the rate of approximately 22 each week.

One of my chapels was in the village of Middleton-by-Wirksworth. One of the oldest ladies in the village told me that when she was much younger, on Sunday mornings when the Methodists were still in bed she would go round with a long pole and knock on their upstairs windows to get them up in time for church. Sometimes when I was preaching in the chapel, I could hear loud explosions coming from the nearby quarry. Hundreds of tons of stone was quarried from it and used in the building of the Bank of England in London.

A few miles away was the rather drab town of Wirksworth. The Methodist Chapel of which I had pastoral charge had a small glass case containing the bonnet of the author of *Adam Bede*, George Eliot, who in her book describes graphically the Methodists and the country around Sir Richard Arkwright's mills.

One of the delightful occasions at Wirksworth was the blessing of the wells during the month of May, a ceremony in which I shared each year. Here a spring of water was particularly important when there were seasons of drought, and especially at the time of the plagues from medieval times to the seventeenth century. The custom grew up of adorning the wells with thousands of petals set in clay within a wooden frame, depicting a scene from the Bible.

Derbyshire, with its breathtaking scenery and its lovely walks through the dales, was a wonderful place to begin my ministry and, inexperienced as I was, I cannot thank God enough for the kindness, encouragement, and generosity of the people in the churches for which I had pastoral care. All too soon my two years as a pre-collegiate probationer came to an end and I was sent to Hartley Victoria Theological College in September 1948 to continue with my studies. It was hard to leave Betty and the Home Farm, which had been my home for over a year, to go to the city of Manchester, but I had so much to look forward to in the theological studies, and I would also have opportunity to return to Willersley when I was on holiday.

My two years in Derbyshire went quickly, but I learned a great deal about the circuit ministry and the country people so devoted to their chapels. The Derbyshire people gave me generous hospitality and their wisdom, example, and inspiration would always be remembered. The two years I had in the Matlock Trinity Circuit was a foretaste of heaven. It was with some trepidation, therefore, that I left the castle to start upon another adventure in my training.

Chapter Six

College

Manchester was an unknown city for me. My brother, Stanley, was trained at Hartley Victoria Theological College and so I was following in his footsteps. Over the wrought iron gates of the college was its motto in Latin: "Ubi Spiritus Ibi Libertas", meaning "Where the Spirit is there is liberty". The principal, Reverend Dr Henry Meecham, greeted all the new students in the main lecture room and introduced the members of the teaching staff, who sat in their gowns. He began by saying: "From now on gentlemen, it will be plain living and high thinking." Certainly, it was plain living; we had our daily share of Hartley's jam because the benefactor was Sir William Hartley, after whom the college was named. There was also a large rhubarb patch and we had more than our share of that. Matron thought it was a good thing to keep students healthy, and that rhubarb would do the trick! Whether all of us students engaged in high thinking is another matter. We were a motley crowd, most of whom had not long been out of the services.

I enjoyed listening to the lectures on the art of preaching and hearing students preach in the college chapel and then attending the sermon class to make observations on the sermon, its content and presentation. I remember with affection our homiletics teacher and his words of advice: "Let Christ be the diamond to shine in the bosom of all your sermons." I owe more than I can say to Hartley Victoria College and all the tutors. They taught me me how to go about gaining the requisite knowledge to equip me for a life's ministry. It was there that I gained an insight into the philosophy of religion, an interest which began in earlier years in conversation with my local church organist, and New Testament Greek, in which the principal was an expert, being a Doctor of Divinity of Manchester University. The Old Testament tutor, Yeoman Muckle, taught me to love the Old Testament and to begin the study of Hebrew in preparation for the Batchelor of Divinity degree. He used to say that a man preparing for the ministry needs to have a reasonable knowledge of the scriptures, if possible in the original languages. It puzzled him that anyone should put B.D. after his name without being able to say that he could at least understand what Paul or Isaiah actually said in the first place. And one most important thing he said was that as long as Christianity remains a historical religion, Biblical studies will need to be taken seriously. My tutors gave me a thirst for such studies that has remained with me ever since. "The well is deep," the Reverend J. K. Elwood, of the Clapton Mission which I attended as a boy, so frequently said.

Dr Percy Scott, tutor in Religious Philosophy, led classes that were not only stimulating but inspiring. Our text book was: *The Philosophical Approach to Religion* by Dr Eric S. Waterhouse, a book that I regarded as a little gem and to which I have turned again and again in my ministry.

It was at Hartley College that I made life-long friends: Sam Connolly, captain of the football team, but a lover of Christ and a great mission man; John Creber, who went into the Royal Navy and became Principal Chaplain, receiving the CBE for his work in the Navy; George Beck, who in those earlier days in college made me laugh a lot and was a good friend; and Eric Bryant, who died far too early in his ministry, but who left his mark upon all of us in our tea club.

Chapter Seven

Walton-on-Thames: Royal Army Chaplains' Department

I found the studies and examinations very testing but it was a joy to make frequent returns to Willersley to see Betty, to whom I became engaged. While in college I kept up my hobby of painting and painted a large oil painting of John Wesley, after Frank Salisbury.

With the completion of my college training, the Methodist Conference sent me to Walton-on Thames. I lived in Chertsey, a beauty spot close by the River Thames, with two maiden ladies, well into their sixties, who looked after me and spoiled me with their excellent cooking. They became great friends and encouraged my ministry to the people of the Methodist Church in Chertsey, and my other churches at Addlestone, Weybridge, and Shepperton, all within a short distance of Chertsey. I felt that Millie and Dorothy, as they were named, were soul partners, kindred spirits. We had long discussions at meal times on most aspects of Christianity. Millie, the elder of the two sisters said to me after a discussion on the meaning of love, "How wonderful it will be to be in heaven to love each other without being misunderstood." These two gracious souls were Quakers; to me they were the salt of the earth, and I loved them dearly.

Betty and Allan (engagement)

I remained in the Walton-on-Thames circuit until 1951, when I felt the call to serve as a Chaplain to the Forces. My first love was the Royal Air Force, having served during the war in that branch of the services, but there was no vacancy in the RAF. However, one occurred in the army, and I was accepted by the Royal Navy, Army and Air Force Board of the Methodist Church and recommended for a commission to the army authorities. I was given a short service commission for six years, and my name appeared in the *London Gazette* as a commissioned officer in the Royal Army Chaplains' Department of the Land Forces from the first day of October 1951. Shortly after, I received the official document, given at the Court of St James's, "By His Majesty's Command", signed by the King, GEORGE R.

After obtaining all the necessary uniform in the rank of Captain, I proceeded to Bagshot Park in Surrey, the Royal Army Chaplains' Department Centre. Bagshot Park is on the southern tip of Windsor Great Park, about an hour's run from London. Until his death in

January 1942 it was the home of the Duke of Connaught. The house stood in 40 acres of beautiful grounds, which included well cared for gardens. Prior to 1939 the RAChD was the only corps in the British Army that had no depot or permanent headquarters. Late in 1946 the house was offered to the Chaplain General of the Royal Army Chaplains' Department by HM King George V1, to to be used as a Church House and Chaplains' depot. The total estate of about 320 acres, including the park where the house was situated, contained many rare specimens of shrubs and trees planted by the Duke of Connaught himself. The house was leased to the army at a nominal rent; the Crown having the option to terminate the lease should the house be required as a residence for any children of the sovereign.

All clergymen who were given commissions to serve in the army as chaplains were required to attend a three week course that included attendance at the Royal Military Academy, Sandhurst. I found it quite a strenuous course, which included a great deal of physical training, running over a mapped out course, map reading, and being drilled by a Sergeant Major who, though he put us through our paces, always referred to us as "gentlemen".

The first thing to catch my eye when I entered the house was the oak mantelpiece in the entrance hall, on which was a large replica of the Chaplains' badge, a Maltese Cross bearing the words, "In this sign conquer". Apparently, the Roman Emperor Constantine, in a battle round about 312 AD, had seen the cross of Jesus athwart in the midday sun inscribed with the words: "By this conquer". The battle was won, and Constantine came to believe, with the aid of the God of the Christians. Eusebius, the historian, wrote: "Throughout the world a bright and glorious day, an unclouded brilliance, illuminated all the churches of Christ with a heavenly light." After the victory Constantine granted freedom to Christians to practise their religion and restored to the church the legal right to hold property. This was an enormous step forward.

A story is told that when the badge for the Army Chaplains was designed and presented to the king for approval, the motto: "In this sign conquer", was in Latin. The king very quickly said that the motto should be in English, so that every soldier would be able to

Chaplain General, The Reverend Canon Victor Pike (centre), at Bagshot Park, with chaplains. I am on the far right, back row.

understand it. And so it was transcribed into English, and every chaplain has the badge on his cap.

The house had what was originally called: "The Salon"; it contained the various trophies and souvenirs collected by the Duke of Connaught during his military service and tours overseas; this was divided to form the Memorial Chapel and the museum. Morning prayers and Compline were held in the chapel.

I was told by the Departmental Secretary that, at the age of twenty-eight, I was the youngest chaplain at that time in the army.

King's Regulations stated: "Chaplains will be treated with the respect due to their rank and profession, and Commanding Officers will render them every assistance in carrying out their duties", and this was my experience with each of the Commanding Officers I was privileged to serve under.

I found the course to be enjoyable, as did most of the chaplains, and I loved the fellowship we had together. On the last day of the course, the Chaplain General, Victor Pike, an Anglican Clergyman, gave an address in the chapel. I recall him referring to William Temple, a great twentieth century Archbishop of Canterbury, who said: "No man can be won for the Kingdom of God by argumentation." He ended his address by saying "Love your men, and they will love you. Their entrance to the Kingdom of Heaven will only be achieved by God's love operating through you."

As it was known that I was shortly to be married, a collection was taken for me to buy a wedding present. It was a kind gesture. Before leaving Bagshot Park I received my posting orders. They were headed "War Office", and continued, "You will proceed on two weeks embarkation leave before going to Hong Kong to be chaplain in the garrison." The posting instructions accelerated our marriage plans, all of which were hastily arranged by Betty. I left Bagshot Park and once again took up residence at Willersley Castle. The date of our wedding was fixed for the 7th November 1951. In the days leading up to our marriage I had to go to the military tailors in London to get kitted out for overseas service, which included tropical kit and dress uniform. I recall, as a boy, seeing the notice: "Join the army and see the world". I had no idea that one day I would do just that, as a chaplain in the King's army. God does certainly move in a mysterious way.

Chapter Eight

Ordination, Hong Kong

At the June Methodist Conference, 1951 I was ordained; it marked the culmination of my studies in college and the probationary period I had in Matlock Trinity and Walton-on-Thames circuits. My ordination took place in Sheffield; the service was impressive and moving, particularly when I was handed a Bible and the President said: "Receive this Bible as a sign of the authority committed to you this day to preach the word of God and celebrate the sacraments. Serve the needy. Minister to the sick. Welcome the stranger.Seek the lost." And so with my ordination and my training as a chaplain at Bagshot Park over I was ready to take up my active ministry.

Our wedding day was a happy occasion. My brother Stanley was best man and Betty's two brothers were the ushers. We were married at Rosehill Methodist Church, Derby, by my former chairman of the Derby District, The Reverend John Swarbrick, a dear friend to both of us. The preparation for our wedding had to be hurried due to my overseas posting to Hong Kong, but my parents-in-law gave us a wonderful reception, after which we made our way to London and stayed at the Cumberland Hotel. We spent our honeymoon in Bournemouth and I spent the last few days at Willersley, where we met in 1947, with Betty.

Allan and Betty: wedding day, 7th November 1951

Betty came to see me off at Matlock Station and after our good-byes we were separated for almost three years. My father met me at Waterloo Station to say goodbye and gave me some friendly advice, speaking as an old soldier who knew so much about the army. As I look back on those years I wonder how I managed to endure the long separation. But I also knew that many of the men who were proceeding overseas with me also left wives behind them for a long period of separation.

I embarked on a cold wet night on the *Empire Orwell*, the troop-ship that was to take me and several hundred soldiers to Hong Kong and some to Korea. The ship sailed on the evening tide from Southampton. I had time to telephone Betty and tell her that all was well and that I would write to her at every port of call. There was something of excitement about this voyage. Everything was new and there was a lot of interest to occupy my mind but I missed Betty dreadfully and longed to be with her.

There was brass plaque over the Purser's office bearing the words: "This is a Strength through Joy ship, captured by the Royal Navy from the German Navy, used to give holidays to the wives and families of serving soldiers". There were two other chaplains with me on board, a Baptist and an Anglican. We arranged Padres' Hours and services during the week and Sundays. The voyage was scheduled to take twenty-eight days. Soon after we reached the Mediterranean we came into warm weather and were able to put away our winter clothes. I used Psalm 139 as a study for Padres' Hours during the voyage. It seemed appropriate, especially verse 9: "If I take the wings of the morning and dwell in the uttermost part of the sea, even there thy hand shall lead me, and thy right hand shall hold me". I had no idea what it would be like to live in Hong Kong. I found it amusing when we stopped at Port Said and an Egyptian man came on board to perform tricks and sell his wares.

We spent Christmas Day in the Red Sea, where a combined service was held on deck and hundreds of soldiers gathered to sing Christmas carols before being provided with a Christmas dinner of roast turkey and Christmas pudding, served by the officers. It seemed strange to be eating turkey and Christmas pudding in such sweltering heat. We passed through the Gulf of Aden into the Arabian Sea and stopped at the port of Columbo where I had the good fortune to spend several hours with one of our missionaries and his wife and to enjoy their hospitality. We sailed through the Indian Ocean and the Straits of Malacca, calling at Singapore. By this time the atmosphere was very humid. It was good to have an English tea at the famous Raffles Hotel. We passed many islands through the South China Sea and some three hundred miles from Hong Kong I saw a junk with red sails. We landed at Kowloon port, just twenty-eight days from the time we left Southampton. It was the 5th of January 1952 and quite warm, as warm as any August day in England.

As the troopship drew alongside Kowloon wharf I noticed from the boat deck where I was standing ferry boats plying between the mainland and the island. Lots of junks were anchored along the waterfront and I marvelled at a family of Chinese assembled on a junk, with the washing hanging on a line and excited children and animals gathered there. Young boys dived into the water for coins as they were thrown from the decks of the troopship. Quickly they surfaced with smiles and shouts: "More coins . . . more coins." The water appeared to be deep green and everywhere there was activity. When I disembarked I noticed red double decker buses the same as in the the UK and also the London type taxi, along with lines of rickshaws waiting for customers. I felt immensely privileged to have been posted to the colony, but I wondered just how long I would be serving in this first appointment. A military band played on the quay; officers and men dressed in tropical kit waited for instructions to disembark. It was refreshing to step once again on to terra firma after the twenty-eight days ocean journey, albeit we did go ashore at the various ports. But now I had reached my journey's end and I was glad to have arrived safely.

I was interested to see that everything in Kowloon seemed very British and in a way I felt at home. I was met by the Deputy Assistant Chaplain General and given a warm welcome, and also by the Methodist Missionary Society representative, Peter Phillipson. We went to the Naafi Club where we had tea and I was told by the senior chaplain that I would be stationed in the New Territories with the 1st Battalion, The Royal Ulster Rifles, an Irish Regiment that had seen active service in Korea. My overall responsibility was to have pastoral care of Methodist soldiers in the colony. A young soldier was waiting in a jeep to take me and my gear up to the Ulster Rifles' camp. We sped along the Nathan Road and into the open countryside. At one time beyond the Nathan Road the mysteries of China were said to have existed, where bandits and tigers lurked and where unspeakable things went on in the opium dens, but by the 1920s the New Territories were regarded more as a place for enjoyable walking and picnicking. Once away from the town the road twisted and turned through the hills and mountains by reservoirs and endless paddy fields. It took one hour for us to arrive just beyond the village of Fanling, close to the border, where the Royal Ulster Rifles' camp was. The long journey from Southampton was over.

The officers' quarters were arranged in rows of Nissen huts. Each had a white-washed front. Inside was an iron bed covered with a mosquito net, a neat chest of drawers, and a desk. A large fan hung from the ceiling, which was just as well, since I found the heat unbearable. The officers' mess was an old Chinese house about a mile across a golf course, once the home of a wealthy Chinese. On my way to the mess I saw an elderly woman burning joss sticks and a farmer wading through mud behind water buffalo pulling a plough. A description of this farmer fits a verse I came across in Chinese literature: "When the sun rises I work, When the sun sets I rest. I dig the well to drink. I plough the field to eat".

At evening dinner Colonel Drummond, the Commanding Officer, welcomed me in the name of the regiment. Already I felt at home; the officers were friendly and the food was excellent. We were waited upon by Chinese servants dressed in white whose manners were impeccable. The battalion had seen service in Korea and had received lots of casualties. Many were killed and others taken into captivity in Northern Korea. The battalion was on a rest period for recuperation and their numbers were being made up by men from Ireland. They would not be returning to Korea.

When I returned to my quarters it was dark but I could hear a cacophony of music coming from Fanling village, a place that later on I found to be immensely interesting.

A key figure in the 1st Battalion, the Royal Ulster Rifles, was the Sergeant-Major. He was a rough diamond if ever there was one. I felt sorry for the men as he put them through their paces, but there was another side to him that I discovered when he told me how he became a believer in the power of prayer. The incident happened in the heat of the battle in Korea when the Royal Ulster Rifles were in retreat. He said: "Prayer never meant anything to me, Padre, until the Battalion was in full retreat in Korea. I was dressed in full pack, my rifle slung across my back. The Communists were hot on our heels. Some of the companies were in deep trouble. We'd been fighting all night. The Colonel gave orders to pull out and every man to make his way back to a safe zone as quick as possible. We kept moving through the rice fields. Bullets were whistling through the air and mortar shells falling around us. I kept urging the men on, some of the lads were falling down on the roadside exhausted, they couldn't go another step. I was panting for dear life and I felt I must fall down where I was. I bit the earth and in the fields of mud I prayed to God with all my heart, 'O God, help me!' At that moment I felt as though someone had put out their hand and I was being pulled to my knees. Soon I was on my feet and moving fast. I never stopped until I reached a safe area. Once there I was met by other members of the Battalion, but when we took the roll call many were missing, some dead and others taken prisoner. I believe that God answered my prayer. It taught me a lesson, Padre, I shall not wait for another emergency before I pray."

Each morning a Royal Ulster trumpeter standing close to my hut sounded the reveille. I did not need an alarm clock during my two years' stay with the regiment. The music master had his accommodation close by and he was the leader of the Royal Ulster Rifles band. On dinner nights held in the officers' mess the band played during dinner and afterwards in the ante-room. Listening to the band and the pipers was a real treat.

The regiment numbered around one thousand men. They were divided into companies and platoons. Each company had a Company Commander, with the rank of major, and each platoon a subaltern, with the rank of lieutenant. I soon got to know the officers and their various responsibilities. I made a friend of the doctor because he kept me aware of how to avoid various complaints, so easily caught in the New Territories. The malaria mosquito was present where we were and to avoid catching this disease we had to sleep under a mosquito net and also to take a Paludrine tablet (a brand name for the anti-malarial drug) every day.

For many generations Hong Kong was notorious for being one of the most unhealthy places in the British Empire. The fearful epidemics had long since been kept at bay, but the sanitation was virtually non-existent. There were no water closets, so we had to make do with the Elsan portable chemical lavatory. It was always amusing to see Chinese coolies, dressed in black and wearing large broad-brimmed hats, carrying the Elsan buckets on long bamboo poles across their shoulders, one bucket hanging from each end, finely balanced. The contents were liquefied and used for fertilizing the rice paddy fields. My batman told me when I remarked upon the smell that the best rice was grown there. It was noticeable at meal times that all the vegetables had been washed in potassium permanganate, which didn't improve the taste. There was no fresh milk, but one soon got used to the food routine and made the best of it. We were warned by the doctor never to buy fruit from the vendors' stalls, some of which were parked near the entrance to the regiment's camp. Venereal disease was rife among the Chinese women in the dance halls, the nearest of which was at Fanling. One of the problems facing the Colonel of the regiment was the number of men going sick with venereal disease. The Colonel, doctor and I had long discussions at that time as to whether condoms should be issued free to the men at the medical centre. From time to time we took turns in addressing the men on the subject of venereal disease, how to avoid it, how to resist the temptation, and how to live good and healthy lives.

One of my duties was to interview "Asian Ladies", as they were officially called, who wished to marry soldiers in the regiment. It was necessary to get a missionary representative who knew the language to act as my interpreter when I had to interview such ladies. It was my responsibility to protect the men from making a grave mistake that they would come to regret. I had sixteen applications for marriage during my two year stay with the regiment and I found it quite impossible to perform a marriage ceremony for any of the applicants. The Colonel supported me and would not sign any application form to permit a marriage to take place. In some cases the Colonel solved the problem by having the man in question posted to Singapore. This procedure took place in other regiments too, until the War Office in London got to hear about it and an instruction was sent to commanding officers that they must not in future post soldiers from Hong Kong to Singapore to avoid such marriages taking place. Financially, these Asian Ladies, if married, would be far better off by virtue of having the marriage allowance.

I made a friend of the Quartermaster who was always helpful in obtaining equipment for the regimental chapel. When I became a chaplain I was issued with what I called a "portable church"; it consisted of a small leather suitcase that contained a communion set and cross and a supply of paperback hymn books. It was, therefore, possible to set up a church and administer the sacraments in the field.

As far as it was possible I joined in the activities of the regiment. One such activity was a must for all ranks, including the doctor and the chaplain. By order of the Commanding Officer all those under thirty-five years of age had to go on a cross-country run every Friday afternoon, unless they had a dispensation from the Medical Officer. The route was marked out for us and at the sound of the Colonel's whistle the cross-country run began. The local Chinese families turned out to watch us start. I wondered what they thought of this exercise. The doctor and I kept together but we were always the last to return, much to the amusement of many of the other ranks who cheered us in as we came through the regimental entrance gates. After the run a glass of ice-cold squash was as nectar from heaven!

Every Sunday morning I took a service in the cinema, which on Sundays was used as a church. Anyone who wished to attend was welcome. Church parades, apart from special occasions such as St Patrick's Day were no longer compulsory. I never liked compulsory church parades when I served in the RAF during the war. The cinema was comfortable and a piano was available. It was always a joy to hear men singing. As far as possible I had men sharing in the service, reading the lessons, and sometimes taking the prayers.

Lunch in the mess on Sundays was always special, usually a very hot curry, which I enjoyed. The Chinese cook was excellent and the food was of a very high standard. After lunch I drove my car down to Kowloon and took it on the ferry across the harbour, known as "Fragrant Harbour"; the twinkling lights at night made it a veritable fairyland. My destination was the Methodist Sailors' and Soldiers' Home, where I stayed until Monday morning. From time to time I conducted the Sunday evening service in the English Methodist Church in Wanchai. This district of Hong Kong was known as the red light area, and was out of bounds to the soldiers unless they were attending the church service. After the service I returned to the Home, where community hymn singing was arranged for all ranks, followed by tea and cakes. It was a popular evening and especially for the men of the Royal Navy who were on shore leave for forty-eight hours. The

Wanchai District was patrolled by the Military Police. The soldiers and sailors had a ditty: "Way down in Wanchai there is a place of fame. / There stands a street, and Lockhart is its name. / Slant-eyed Chinese maidens all around I see, / Calling out 'Artillery man, abide with me'".

Sometimes I would stay with a Methodist family up in the Peak. This was always very special and I enjoyed the home comforts, and especially the air-conditioning that, in the hot season, was most welcome. The Peak was well known as a beautiful residential area, the hillsides being lined with ferns and shrubs, and the view of the harbour was breathtaking. On my way back to the regiment I would call on Methodist soldiers stationed in other units of the army. In some respects the colony was like a large Methodist circuit, the units like churches. In one unit I met Geoffrey Senior, who was a candidate for our ministry, and I was able to help him in his preparation for the ministry of the Methodist Church.

After his acceptance and training he returned to the colony in 1974, where he was Methodist Schools' Chaplain and Supervisor until 1981. He also served in other parts of South-East Asia, became fluent in Chinese, and in his own right became an authority on Chinese church affairs.

During my stay in the colony I received a number of men into the membership of the Methodist Church and I also held Moral Leadership Courses in the Sailors' and Soldiers' Home.

One of the wonders of the regiment was the large marquee tent that housed the tailor's shop, the laundry, and the clothing repair shop. I was measured for a grey suit one Monday morning, cut and fitted the next day, and my made-to-measure suit was ready to wear on Sunday. The Chinese workers could make most things and their work was of a high quality. Laundry was gathered on Monday mornings, and returned in a neat bundle by mid-week to my quarter. I was not amused, however, when I visited the marquee tent to find an amah ironing a shirt. At the end of the ironing board was a cup, from which she took a sip and squirted it on the shirt collar. I discovered, when enquiring from my batman, that the cup contained starch! Be that as it may, the all-purpose work tent had its uses. It was put to full stretch on the day before St Patrick's Day. The Colonel called me into his office and showed me the special casket of shamrock that had been flown from Ireland, enough to give each man on parade at the St. Patrick's Day service a piece of shamrock from the wife of the Brigade Commander. The flight, which took thirty-six hours, was too much for the shamrock, which was a heap of limp pieces unfit for distribution next day. "What shall we do, Padre?", he asked. I told him I thought the tailor in the all-purpose work tent would help. And without delay I went to him, told him of our problem, drew a piece of shamrock and asked him if he could make a thousand pieces of shamrock before eight o'clock next morning. He smiled and said that it could be done and I could collect the shamrock at that time. I went and assured the Colonel that all would be well, pointing out, furthermore, that the men could keep the shamrock as a souvenir of the occasion. Next morning, with some trepidation, I went to the tent and on several trays were one thousand pieces of shamrock, beautifully made of green material with wire stems. I couldn't believe my eyes; what I thought was impossible had been done. I enquired how it had been accomplished and I was told that thirty amahs worked through the night to get the job done in time. The Colonel was delighted, and during the service the Brigadier's wife handed out the shamrock, a piece for everyone on parade! All went well.

The Chinese were very clever at copying. If you took a hat and asked for a replica it would be copied perfectly. In the many emporiums in Nathan Road, Kowloon, I saw some of their splendid work, the art of paper making, book production, and exquisite carvings in ivory.

Six festivals marked the Chinese New Year. All the shops were closed for three days and over the colony in the villages and in the towns there were ceaseless sounds of fire crackers. But the wonder of wonders was watching the dragon made up of dozens of Chinese men dancing and manoeuvring, to the delight of the hundreds gathered to watch the ceremony. The Chinese dragon, according to one standard description, was a bizarre composition of physical features: it had the head of a camel, the horns of a deer, the neck of a snake, the scales of a carp, the claws of an eagle, and the paws of a tiger. In China these extraordinary living sculptures of dragons, wreathed in grass and creepers, were symbols of vitality and strength. Yet the Feast of Lanterns appealed to me. This was very colourful and beautiful. The shops were filled with lanterns of different sizes and colours. Even the back streets of Wanchai, with their appalling squalor, responded to the magic of the lantern and to the sound of gongs.

Chinese food appealed to me and on one occasion I was invited to a meal with a Chinese family. My hostess was a charming lady and had set out a table with lots of delightful sea foods, chicken slices, hard-boiled eggs, grated carrots, sliced apples and much more. Beside each plate was a rice bowl and chopsticks. Imagine my embarrassment when all were seated around the table and I took up my chopsticks and tried to emulate the members of the family. Of course it was impossible, and I had to overcome my embarrassment and ask for a knife, fork and spoon. The chopstick art was not for me, but I was more than at home when I turned over the knife and saw the words: "Made in Sheffield".

Happy Valley in Hong Kong was famous for its racecourse. The Chinese were great gamblers, but many a Chinese seeking fortune had been ruined at Happy Valley. For me this name had another meaning, for it was here in a large cemetery that we laid to rest one of the subaltern officers who was killed in an accident. He had just joined the regiment after completing his training at Sandhurst. On the Sunday before his death I asked him to read the lesson at the morning service. On Tuesday he went in his Land Rover to inspect an outpost high up on a promontory overlooking the Chinese border. The route he took was a dangerous one and out of bounds to all drivers. In a split second of misjudgment his Land Rover went over the side of the promontory and dropped hundreds of feet to lodge on some rocks. He was killed instantly. The entire regiment attended the funeral, which I conducted at Happy Valley cemetery. He was buried with full military honours. The Pipe Major played a lament and when I said the words of committal, the buglers sounded the Last Post and the Reveille. A volley of shots echoed over Happy Valley and we returned to our camp in the New Territories. Such sad events as these I never forgot.

Life in the officers' mess was never dull, especially on the dinner nights when we wore dress uniform for dinner. The mess table was set out with a number of silver trophies inscribed with past battles in which the Royal Ulster Rifles had been engaged. On dinner nights a VIP was invited. During my stay with the regiment we had the Governor of Hong Kong, the Archbishop of Canterbury, and the Chaplain General. If a famous film star came to visit the troops he, too, would be invited A lesser but well known personality, a comedian called Charlie Chester, sat next to me on one occasion and after dinner gave me a copy of a poem that he had written in the Second World War, entitled "Pass Friend, All's Well".

"So you've come to the end of your journey, soldier?
and you say you've been brave and true?
Well they're not the qualities I need my friend,
before I can pass you through.
You say that you've merits outstanding in battle and righteous
    wars must be won,
But have you had courage to pray to the Lord, for the sins that
    you need not have done?
You pause at my challenge dear soldier,
Of weapons I've none in my hand,
For I am the sentry, Saint Peter, and this is my Maker's own
    land.
And to pass to the life everlasting, you must prove beyond
    word of all doubt,
Whether or no you're our friend or our foe,
To find sanctuary here or cast out.
You seem not afraid at my quest,
There's no need to answer me soldier, I can see that your soul
    is at rest.
And for courage and loyalty, soldier, in resisting the talons of
    hell,
We offer, not medals, but peace everlasting, soldier.
Pass friend, all's well."

It has been said that if you can drive in Hong Kong you can drive anywhere, and so I purchased a new car to use in the colony for my personal use. One Sunday afternoon I took it across on the ferry to the island. All went well until I realized I was going up a one-way street and in a split second had to apply my brakes because coming towards me was a car driven by a Chinese. It was one of those cars that has been described as "a coughing, spluttering, honking demon". Before I could say "Jack Robinson" we met with some force. Fortunately, neither of us was injured but my new car was damaged to the sum of four hundred Hong Kong dollars. Of course, I was in the wrong. We exchanged our names, cards for insurance purposes, and fortunately we were both able still to drive our cars. I had to report it to the police and in due course I received a summons for going the wrong way up a one-way street. My Colonel, with his tongue in his cheek, said he would visit his chaplain in prison. It was no joke because the police came down very hard on traffic offences, and a prison sentence was often given to those who broke the law. However, the weeks went by and I heard no more, until one Sunday morning, just before I was about to take the morning service, a smooth-faced, smart Chinese constable, riding on an immaculate motorbike handed me an envelope. It was a summons for me to appear in court to answer the charge. I was advised to write a letter to the magistrate, pleading guilty to the traffic offence, instead of appearing in court. Fortunately for me the Colonel knew the magistrate and in due course I was fined the sum of one Hong Kong dollar, much to my relief. I was careful after that incident to drive with great caution.

There was another occasion that I was involved with the police, when I was driving up the Nathan Road and pulled up quickly to allow a Chinese lady to cross the busy road, but this time I was not in the wrong. A Chinese on a motorbike went straight into my rear bumper as I applied my brakes and to my astonishment shot over the top of my car and somehow landed on his feet in front of my car. When a policeman arrived as if from nowhere he asked the motorcyclist if he was all right, and he nodded his head. And then the policeman arrested him because he had no driving licence, no insurance, and in fact was only a learner. I never heard what happened to him but it would certainly have been a prison sentence.

The most difficult endurance test whilst I was in the New Territories was the climate. It could be terribly hot and humid and on a Sunday when I was taking a service my cassock was soaked with perspiration. It was necessary every day to shower at least three times, except in the autumn when the weather was cool. When it was very hot one longed for the night time, when it became more bearable. There was no air-conditioning in the New Territories but visiting some of my English friends in the Peak was a heavenly experience for all of them had air-conditioning. No one with any sense would stay around longer than necessary on a baking hot day. As Noel Coward put it so aptly: "At twelve noon the natives swoon, and no further work is done / But mad dogs and Englishmen go out in the midday sun". The monsoon period was trying. It rained continually for weeks at a time. Many of the squatter settlements were washed away from the hillsides. All the junks and sampans anchored inshore when there was a hurricane. Large ocean-going vessels went into Hong Kong Bay, and faced the storm with engines full on, so I have been told. The hurricanes were given ladies' names, such as Dorothy, or Matilda, and it was said this was because, like ladies, the hurricanes were unpredictable! Later on men's names were also given to hurricanes.

From the window of my quarter I could see in the distance the mountains of Communist China. From time to time I was taken in a jeep by a platoon commander to visit one of our outposts that overlooked the border. With fieldglasses it was possible to see the Communist soldiers playing football. The platoon commander made sure that the defences were strong, and those on duty supplied with ample food and ammunition. The role of the Royal Ulster Rifles' Regiment was to patrol the border.

I recall going up to the border to the village of Sha Ta Kok; surely there is no other village like this anywhere in the world. In this village China–England Street marks the demarcation of the frontier. One row of stone pots down the centre of the street gave a clear indication of what has been the frontier since 1898. Nearby was Lu Wu station, where the trains passed under a steel bridge into China proper. At the time I was stationed with the Royal Ulster Rifles no one was allowed over the border into China, and anyone attempting to do so was liable to be shot.

I was told that at night the Roman Catholic priest who was stationed at Fanling would go over the border and give Holy Communion to relatives of those who lived in Fanling. It was fraught with danger but he was prepared to take the risk. When I heard of this I decided to pay him a visit. I had seen him riding a two stroke motor-cycle, wearing a black cassock and with a black biretta on his head. He was often surrounded by children and I was told that he was greatly loved. I was directed to where he lived, a small building in the market place. I went through a door made of bamboo sticks, and was met by a smell of garlic and fish. Along a corridor I entered a dark room, cluttered with trinkets and carved boxes. At one end I saw an altar covered with a white linen cloth on which was a silver crucifix. A smell of incense pervaded the house. Sitting near the altar was the priest. His hair was greying at the sides and his hollow cheeks made him look frail. I felt I was in the presence of a holy man of God. He took my hand and gave me a warm welcome, speaking in English but with an Italian accent. He asked me what my denomination was. He told me he was born in Italy but had come to the New Territories many years ago. He learned the language of Hakka, the language of the fishing folk. I asked him how far his parish stretched and he said from Fanling to the other side of the border. He told me what I had already heard, that he went over the border at night to give Holy Communion to relatives of his church family and if he had been caught going over the border he would have been shot on sight. It was a dangerous mission but he was prepared to live dangerously for the Lord. He told me that all the missionaries had come out of China but the people had not lost their faith in God, and one day he believed China would again welcome priests of all denominations.

In Fanling there was an orphanage run by two English ladies. Paddy fields covered every inch of the ground around the orphanage. The heat on the day I visited the orphanage was intense. I was made welcome and had afternoon tea in the lounge. After tea the children were gathered together in the main hall and they sang a hymn I used to sing as a boy in Sunday School.

> "Jesus bids us shine with a pure, clear light,
> Like a little candle burning in the night:
> In the world is darkness,
> So we must shine;
> You in your small corner, and I in mine".

These small children did actions and pointed to me when they sang "You in your small corner". That was a moment of enlightenment. That afternoon was the first of many visits. I was told that babies were frequently found on the doorstep of the orphanage or even in the rice fields. Professor Butterfield in his book *Christianity and History* wrote:

> These people work more wisely who seek to achieve good in their own small corner of the world and then leave the leaven to leaven the whole lump, than those who are for ever thinking that life is vain unless one can act through the central government, carry legislation, achieve political power and do big things.
>
> Butterfield, *Christianity and History*

The work in the orphanage was hard and the two young ladies needed not only their spiritual energies, but also every ounce of physical strength. Their courage and faith was an enormous example to me as I went about my duties.

The battalion doctor, an orthodox Jew, would send soldiers to me if he thought I could be of help. One problem soldiers had to face was depression, which brought some to the sick room for treatment. I was responsible for all welfare matters and spent a lot of my time writing to families. I arranged Padres' Hours and discussion groups, and helped with sporting activities. We had a boxing ring erected in the camp and I found it interesting to watch, but it was a sport that needed careful oversight and I did not believe in professional boxing. Boredom was a real problem, and for some men serving thousands of miles away from home was too much for them. It was important to get them interested in things beyond the path of everyday duty, and so there were art classes, bird watching, gardening, and a library to help keep up their morale.

During the two years I spent with the battalion we were engaged in supporting the police in dealing with riots in Kowloon. This was a frightening experience, but fortunately there were only few casualties and the riots were firmly put down. One of the Ulster Rifles' soldiers got himself in serious trouble when, on sentry duty, he shot a Chinese ice cream vendor at the battalion gates. The Chinese vendor died immediately and the soldier was subsequently charged with his murder. He was taken to a prison in Hong Kong and there began a lengthy court case, which was reported in all the Chinese newspapers. I had to visit him in prison and his parents were flown out from Ireland. It was all very worrying because at that time the death sentence was the penalty for murder and the rifleman in question was certain he was going to die, and if that were to happen I would, as chaplain, be expected to attend the hanging. There were long discussions in court on the subject of provocation, diminished responsibility, and whether it was an accident. Did he have a bullet up the spout? If so, was this in accordance with army regulations on the use of firearms. What was the cause of death? Did the soldier believe the Chinese vendor was a threat to the battalion? There was a great deal of coverage in the Irish press. Finally, the man was acquitted, discharged from the army and returned to Belfast. It was a long drawn out affair and I was greatly relieved when it was all over, as indeed were his parents.

On such matters as these I found it extremely hard to give guidance. In army life there were moments of horror at the things men did, especially when under the influence of drink, and the misery that resulted from their actions. One subaltern officer was discharged from the service for forging cheques to pay mess bills that he simply couldn't afford. A major, company commander, an exceptionally nice man, took to the whisky bottle in his room. He'd been in the army for many years, won the Military Cross during the war and served with distinction, but he was in danger of ending his army career. I discovered in conversation with him that he had divorced his wife, only to find he was still in love with her. She was at home in Ireland and the tension within him was almost too much to bear. We had long talks on the power of prayer and to my joy one Sunday I saw him for the first time in church. The major had found God and with it a new peace. He was also able to cope with his domestic problems and get on with his army career. I mention these cases because I was involved in this kind of work and I was chaplain to the soldiers and also to the families of those living in married quarters.

In May 1953 I received orders from the War Office to proceed to Korea. I had been in the colony since January 1951; it was time for me to move on. I was given a farewell dinner by the officers of the Royal Ulster Rifles and the next day the Commanding Officer, Colonel Drummond, and the second in command came with me to the troopship *Empire Orwell* to say farewell. And so I left this undisputed colossus of the East, and one of the world's oldest civilizations. Though my work was mainly with the army, I did get to know something of the Chinese way of life and their cultural pursuits. It has been said that everyone grand and famous comes to Hong Kong. I certainly was neither grand nor famous, but I wouldn't have missed the experience. My one regret was that Betty was unable to be with me in the colony to see for herself something of the extraordinary life of the Chinese, the vast panoply of neon advertisements at night, the famous Nathan Road leading up to the New Territories, and the breathtaking views from high up in the Peak, looking down upon the bay with its anchored great liners, junks, and small fishing boats. And so I said goodbye to Hong Kong as the troopship slowly set sail for Korea, leaving behind a trail of white foam.

Chapter Nine

Korea

While serving in Hong Kong as chaplain to the lst Battalion, The Royal Ulster Rifles, I followed the war in Korea closely. Hundreds of men who came out with me on the troopship *Empire Orwell* went on to Korea. They joined a woefully equipped British contingent and went into battle. Over seven hundred British soldiers died in the Korean War and were buried in the United Nations Cemetery in Pusan. Provision had not been made for the bitter Korean winters. Many men suffered from frostbite as a result of exposing their hands when firing guns.

On Christmas Day 1951 it was 36° below zero. There were no heaters, and stoves had to be made from ammunition cases. Empty ration tins were used to make chimneys so that a fire could be lit in whatever shelters were made. As time went by great improvements were made in the clothing for summer and winter's extreme weather conditions. String vests, long johns, specially protected boots and parkas were provided for each man. One splendid invention was tinned soup that could be automatically heated. I was told how soldiers on duty on bitter nights stayed in makeshift holes in the ground and enjoyed piping hot soup.

The war had begun on the morning of the 25th June 1950, when the North Korean forces opened fire with artillery and mortars upon

United Nations' Cemetery, Pusan

the South Korean positions that faced them across the 38th Parallel. It wasn't long before the South Korean forces were overwhelmed and in full retreat. The fighting had been vicious; thousands of South Korean soldiers had been killed, the American forces had sustained heavy losses, and most of the Gloucester battalion had either been taken into captivity, killed in battle, or made to retreat.

The Reverend Sam Davies, Anglican chaplain to the 1st Battalion the Gloucester Regiment would always be remembered as a chaplain who stayed with his men when many of them, including Colonel Carne, the colonel of the regiment, were taken prisoner by the enemy.

The "Glorious Gloucesters", as they were called, earned the admiration of the free world for their stand against the onslaught of the North Korean and Chinese Communists. Sam Davies spent two and a half years as a prisoner of the North Koreans. His experiences were described in his book *In Spite of Dungeons*. He was the only British chaplain to experience captivity in Communist hands and to have undergone the dreaded indoctrination of the Communists.

While I had been in Hong Kong many of the officers and men of the Royal Ulster Rifles who had served with the Battalion in Korea told me dreadful stories of their experiences in the fighting. At that time I had no idea that I would be going to the war in Korea.

It seemed I was getting used to the troopship *Empire Orwell* because it was on this troopship that I sailed from Southampton to the colony of Hong Kong in November 1951. Then I was bound for a peaceful service station that had not experienced war since the occupation by the Japanese on Christmas Day 1941. Proceeding to Korea, where there had been such fierce fighting, was a daunting experience. I wondered how I would get used to a posting where war was still going on. The stories I heard from those who had served in the Korean war made me think of the preciousness of life and what might happen to me when I arrived there. The journey to Pusan took five days, taking us through the Formosa Strait, into the East China Sea and the Korean Strait. It was an uneventful journey and we finally arrived at the port of Pusan in early June 1953.

My first impression of Korea was as I stood on the top deck of the troopship on a rather dull Sunday afternoon. No way could I think of it as "Land of the morning calm", its true name. As I saw Pusan then it seemed to be a land of ugliness ravaged by war.

Two tugs pulled the troopship into her berthing place at the Pusan dock. Several small ships were anchored in the bay and two Royal Navy ships stood by. A steel crane used for unloading baggage from the ship's hold was on the dockside ready to commence work. Written in large red letters on the side of the crane were the words: "7th Transportation Major Port, the busiest Port in the World".

The British minister and his wife came aboard with Korean army officials to greet us, while two American bands played popular pieces to the applause of all on board. Alongside the bands were the flags of the United Nations. Disembarkation commenced with great speed and soon a whole battalion was being moved by road to the transit camp.

I remained in Pusan for two days, during which time I had my first opportunity of seeing the people of Korea and their living conditions. Hundreds of dwelling places, all of which were the flimsiest of shacks, with little protection from summer's heavy rains or winter's biting winds, were to be found in every conceivable position. In some places there were several families who lived in a tent or shed, and some had nowhere to live; sleeping in cardboard boxes or under bits of canvas they could get from the army. I was told by a reliable authority that most of the people seen on the streets of Pusan were refugees. An American Methodist missionary, who worked with his wife in Korea, told me that there were estimated to be ten million displaced persons in South Korea and half of these were listed as destitute. In spite of these most depressing figures he went on to say the Korean Methodist Church had made a splendid recovery and, though the physical environment depressed visitors, all who heard the singing and saw the spiritual glow of the Korean Christians would be lifted to great spiritual heights.

After my two days in Pusan I took the night train up to Seoul. A military policeman, known as a "Red-cap" showed me to my place in the train, number 72, berth 7 lower, a sleeping compartment. All

Pusan shacks

ranks had to endure hard wooden seats for the journey, which took twelve hours.

The sleeping compartment was dark, but I just couldn't get to sleep. Opposite me was an American businessman on his way to Seoul. From our conversation I assumed he thought the war would soon end and that there were great opportunities for starting up business. My mind, however, was not on his vision for the future, but on the stark reality that, with hundreds of troops, I was going up to the front line. What prospects had I of seeing the war through; would I be killed or taken prisoner?

I tried to sleep but the carriage rocked and the bed was like sleeping on stone. Eventually, I fell into a series of unsatisfactory catnaps. After what seemed an eternity I saw dawn break over the Korean hills, and then the sun rose over the mountains. It was a beautiful sight and at that moment I could understand why Korea was called, "Land of the morning calm".

I felt tired and hungry as the troop train arrived at Seoul station just after 7.30 a.m. The troops poured out of the train carrying their rifles and kit bags, and quickly assembled to be taken by lorries up to the Main Division along the dusty supply route. Seoul station looked as if had seen better days, it was terribly cold, and there were no civilians to be seen anywhere.

I was met by a senior chaplain who took me to the bishop's house next to the cathedral. I was warmly welcomed by the assistant bishop, who told me that I would be staying with him for the next five days before reporting to the 1st Divisional Signals Regiment, where I was to be chaplain. He invited me to have a bath and took me to the bathroom – where there was no bath! It had been taken when the communists first captured Seoul in the summer of 1950. However, in the centre of the room there was a canvas bath large enough for me to sit in cross-legged. A Korean servant brought me hot and cold water in buckets and filled the bath. What a relief to feel clean again. This was my first introduction to roughing it in Korea. Life in Hong Kong was sheer luxury compared with this new experience.

After I had taken my bath the bishop told me that his predecessor, Dr Cooper, had been taken prisoner while he bathed and forced to join a long procession of prisoners, soldiers and civilians, who were made to march to the Yalu River in Northern Korea, some 300 miles from Seoul, led by a communist major who, for his brutality, was named "the mad tiger". Many died on the way, so terrible was the journey.

The bishop and I went to the officers' mess, where there were Korean, Canadian, Australian, New Zealand and British officers. The bishop gave me a conducted tour of the ancient city, where there had been much destruction. The capital building had no windows left and the concrete walls were pitted all over with shell and bullet holes. Seoul was established as a capital city a century before Columbus discovered America. Originally it was surrounded by a ten-mile wall with eight gates, five of which still stood. Within these walls was woven a rich tapestry of cultural history, a history evidenced by the palaces, temples, and monuments that stood there. It was sad to witness the squalor and poverty in this old city, once the dwelling place of the kings. In the market there were stalls full of brass trinkets made from empty shell cases, and a whole variety of brass crosses of various sizes, bells, ashtrays, horseshoes, and vases.

I met another missionary, named Dr Charles Saur, from America. We talked for over an hour about the state of the Methodist Church in Korea. He gave a glowing account of its recovery despite the continuance of the drawn out war. Far from forgetting the church in its hour of need and dire poverty, the Christians turned to the church as never before. The temporary chapels, consisting often of tents or simple buildings with no ceilings and no plaster on the walls and nothing but straw bags on the bare earth to take the place of floors, were crowded every Sunday, both morning and evening, and in most of them a sunrise prayer meeting took place every morning of the year. The church was far from dead. Everywhere the signs were encouraging, though it was obvious from the figures that he quoted that the work would be an uphill climb for years to come.

My stay with the bishop came to an end all too quickly but it was long enough to get acquainted with the situation facing the South Korean government and the weariness of the people with a war that had cost them so far 415,000 soldiers killed with a further 429,000 wounded, and a country whose infrastructure had been destroyed, and millions of its people made homeless and destitute. So far I had not experienced the war at first hand, but I was well aware of the price the 1st Battalion the Royal Ulster Rifles had to pay, since I lived with them for two years.

The journey from Seoul up to the Divisional area was long and tedious, in a jeep that held the dusty road remarkably well. Most of the main supply route, as it was called, was a truck killer, uphill and down, muddy in one place, rocky and dusty in another, full of hairpin curves and deep-pitted holes. But the countryside was at its best on that June morning and in some parts was beautiful. There were miles of paddy fields that probably had been untouched since the war started. As my driver, who so skilfully controlled the jeep, came in sight of the river he exclaimed, "This is the famous Imjin River." From the glimpse I had it looked fast flowing and as wide as the Thames at Waterloo Bridge in London.

Shortly afterwards I arrived at the headquarters of the 1st Divisional Signal Regiment. At that time the war consisted of only skirmishes, and there were signs that an armistice was shortly to take place.

In the matter of a day or two I felt at home, though my sleeping quarter was a small tent dug into the hillside, from which I had a good view of the River Imjin. The Signals Regiment had not previously had a chaplain living with them and so in a sense my work was of a pioneer nature and this excited me. In a short time a large marquee tent was erected as a temporary church and services were held there every Sunday morning until the armistice was signed on the 27th July, 1953 at Panmunjum, just over three years since the war began. The colonel had a splendid idea for a more permanent building for a church and rest centre, a dual purpose building for the benefit of the troops. He outlined his plan for the building that he suggested could be built not far from the River Imjin, where there was a paddy field that the colonel said would provide an excellent spot. And it would be called, "St Martin's", after the regimental church in England, but for our purposes it would be called "St Martin's in the Paddy". The idea won the ready support of the officers and as a follow-up the colonel called me into his caravan to give me the details.

Apparently the colonel had been in touch with his opposite number in the American Signals Division, and discovered that he could supply enough corrugated steel to build a church, a rest room for the men, and also an officers' mess. In exchange for the corrugated steel we would supply their regiment with several lorryloads of tinned butter and jam. However, much thought and planning was necessary before building could take place, and it had to be built before the winter set in. I couldn't help thinking of my college "Hartley Victoria Theological College" affiliated to Manchester University, a splendid place of learning that was founded and built by Sir William Hartley, famous for the manufacture of Hartley's jam. And, believe it or not, here I was in Korea discussing the fact that our regimental church was to be built by providing the Americans with butter and jam! Colonel Starr was enthusiastic about the project and, after some discussion, he invited me to go to Tokyo on what was called "Rest and Refreshment leave", more commonly known as R and R, with the sum of £500. The money was to buy all the necessary equipment for the church and rest room. I was excited at the prospect of going to Tokyo, the largest city in Japan, and even more excited as I wanted to get a small piano and some blue silk to go behind the altar.

In the month of September, when it was already becoming colder, I boarded an American Globemaster plane at Seoul bound for Tokyo. The plane was enormous, large enough to take a London bus, and was packed with troops going on leave. There were five hundred on board, and as we took off I wondered if we would make it over the first mountain range because a member of the crew told me that one had crashed the previous week, resulting in many deaths.

I had always wanted to visit Japan and now my dream was coming true. The centre of Tokyo and in particular the Ginza, the equivalent of Oxford Street in London, was full of colourful shops and emporiums.

Two days after arriving in this extraordinary, busy city I visited the main store, similar to Harrods of London, to spend the money given to me by the colonel. I was introduced to the manager of the store and shown into his office, where I met his young wife and had refreshments. I told the manager I wanted a piano, blue silk for draping behind the altar, candlesticks and vases, tables and chairs. I was shown a catalogue and selected items for the regimental church for shipping to the Royal Signals Regiment within six weeks. I spent the £500 that the colonel had given me and felt satisfied with my purchases.

During my visit I decided to go to Hiroshima, to look around and see for myself the aftermath of the atomic bomb that fell upon the city on 6th August 1945. It was the first atomic bomb to be used in warfare, dropped by the United States of America; the explosion had the force of more than 15,000 tons of TNT, which instantly and completely devastated four square miles of the city of 343,000 inhabitants. Of this number 66,000 were killed and 69,000 were injured, and more than 67% of the structures of the city were destroyed. A woman who sat on a concrete bench at the epicentre of the explosion was incinerated immediately. But in that instant her body obscured the flash of the explosion. One can see the result in the Hiroshima Memorial Museum, a human being reduced to a shadow on a stone!

I spent ten interesting and unforgettable days in Tokyo and one thing I shall never forget was being awakened in my hotel in the middle of the night by a deep rumbling, a sound I had never experienced before in my life. The bed shook and moved sideways, the window frames shuddered and I felt the building move. It was terrifying while it lasted. Thankfully no one was injured, and I was told that the hotel was built on foundations designed for earthquakes and could move several inches in each direction without collapsing.

When I arrived back in the regiment the foundations of the church had already been dug. By early November a large quantity of corrugated steel had arrived from the American regiment and all the materials were available for the erection of the church and officers' mess. The church was designed to be used also as a rest room, and special screens were made for this purpose. A soldier who had experience of altar decoration draped the blue silk on the wall behind the altar. The altar itself was made by a carpenter. It was simple but beautiful, and on it were two brass candlesticks and flower vases made from brass

St Martin's in the Paddy

shell cases. The highly polished brass cross was cut out of an old piece of brass sheeting and mounted on an oak stand. The other church furnishings were made by carpenters in the camp. A brass bell was obtained by one of the officers and every Sunday morning it was rung to call men of the regiment to church. The Australian contingent with the regiment built a huge spire and placed it over the entrance to the church, and a recording of the bells of St Margaret's, Westminster played every Sunday morning, resonating throughout the valley. An artist in the regiment designed a stained glass window of the Madonna and Child, using the colours normally used for painting the vehicles. This beautiful window was inserted in the wall above the altar. After the church was opened Colonel Starr, Commanding Officer, wrote an article in the Royal Corps of Signals magazine, as follows:

> Every Sunday the merry peal of bells echoes across the countryside, followed by the solemn tolling of a solitary bell reminding the regiment that morning service was about to begin. Our chaplain, the Revd. Allan Bowers, turns into the church from welcoming his parishioners as the last note rings out from the steeple and a few moments later the sound of music and voices raised in praise steals out of the entrance, a familiar scene in every town and village throughout the Commonwealth, and finer bell ringing could not be

Madonna and child

heard in London for this is the parish of St Martins. Unfamiliar? Probably you have guessed, this is not Catterick, but the other St Martins, Korea, the Regimental Church of the 1st Commonwealth Divisional Signal Regiment. The bells, a recording of the carillon of St Margaret's Westminster. The Church began when a congregation of seventy-five attended the first service in a tent pitched in a paddy field, on the 11th October, 1953, but even then there was only one name for this Signals church, St Martin's or as the wits would have it, St Martin's in the Paddy!

The church was built on a site in front of the Regimental head-quarters, and facing the parade ground, a warm and comfortable building. It was officially opened on the 20th December, in time for Christmas celebrations. A congregation of over one hundred, officers and men joined in the celebration. From this small beginning had grown a church of which any regiment might be proud, one which even rivaled more elaborate edifices built with Sapper assistance in the Division. The skilful use of screens turned the church into a cheer-ful quiet room when not used for church activities.

The Regiment took great pride in its church and improvements were continually made. A steeple had at the top a "Jimmy", a weather-vane, made by Captain John Colley and the Local Aid Detachment. A stained glass window, painted by Signalman Critchley, a new piano and the usual church fittings provided a splendid atmosphere for wor-ship and praise. A carved prayer desk and oak pews were installed and altar rails were made. Interest spread far beyond Korea and pupils of

Stratford Secondary School fashioned an altar lamp and carved an altar cross for the church and they also embroidered an altar cloth.

The Regiment's enthusiasm was not confined to the appearance of the church but extended to active participation in all its various activities. No persuasion was needed on Sunday mornings when the bright service and lusty singing led by a full choir, and accompanied by Major George Atkins or his relief pianist, the Medical Officer, Lieutenant Ken Sheridan Dawes, always attracted a full congregation. The weekly group and Friday gramophone concerts were regularly attended. Later in the month our mother Church at Catterick would be filled with old comrades and soldiers, and at our service we would be thinking of them and would feel equal pride with them in our Corps Church which we all knew and loved so well, but we would feel additional pride in our own St. Martin's in the Paddy Church, Korea.

A small choir met every Friday evening for practice, led by a sergeant who had been a member of a Welsh Choir. The Quartermaster played the piano and the hymns for the Sunday service were practised. During the week I held a Bible Study Group, attended by officers and men. A Korean Christian also attended, and although he could say only a few words in English he made a valuable contribution to the fellowship. A number of Korean soldiers attached to the regiment were Christians and we were pleased to see them and worship together.

My work as a Methodist Chaplain took me beyond my regiment to various units in the Division. When the Reverend F. W. Hilborne, QHC Deputy Chaplain General, visited us from the War Office, we held a rally that was attended by over one hundred soldiers from all parts of the Divisional area, and after a good tea, a service was held in true Methodist fashion. The singing was the heartiest I had heard since going to Korea, and altogether there was a fine spirit of warm fellowship.

My readers may wonder what the climate was like in Korea. It should be borne in mind that each soldier going to Korea was only allowed to stay for one year and would experience all the seasons of the land. The nation's climate on the whole was temperate, influenced more by being an appendage to the world's largest continent than by the surrounding seas. It can be described as humid, an East Asian monsoon climate. The hottest months were July and August, the coldest December and January. Where the Commonwealth Division was situated, beyond the 38th parallel, near to the northern part of the peninsula, it was bitterly cold during the winter months; Siberia's icy blasts had to be felt to be believed.

When the winter finally came a great transformation took place in the regiment, and all in the space of a few weeks. More and better buildings were erected. Communal quarters, mess halls, recreation rooms, and canteens housed in galvanized huts with glass fibre linings went up with remarkable speed. Tents were improved by the installation of wooden floors, with the outside thoroughly protected by sandbags. The mountains around the valley looked menacing. The River Imjin was completely frozen over and trucks were able to cross from one side of the river to the other, the river being as wide as the Thames at Westminster Bridge. I was told that the resourceful Koreans made good use of the thick ice, cut large slabs and stored them in deep caves, to be sold in the springtime throughout the country.

Every Sunday at 8 a.m. I held a service of Holy Communion open to all ranks and denominations and morning worship was held at 10.30 a.m. Colonel Starr came to both services. I regularly heard him say at the "Officer Groups", "I shall be in church on Sunday and I expect my officers to be there too." There were no compulsory church parades and we had no difficulty in filling the church every Sunday. It was always a joy to see the church full and to hear the bells of St Margaret's, Westminster, which echoed through the valley. In the warmer months we arranged for comfortable chairs to be placed outside the church and the band of one or other of the regiments were invited to give a concert from time to time.

The comfort of the men in the regiment was fully catered for and when off duty the church was opened as a writing and music room. It should be borne in mind that the 25,000 men in the various regiments of the Commonwealth Division were stationed some fifty miles from Seoul across a ten-mile deep stretch of country, rear

River Imjin, Winter 1953

Division to main Division, where there were no civilians and no form of entertainment other than that provided by the regiment or the men themselves. Life could be pretty miserable and boring for some of the soldiers. After the war ended, however, the camp became like a large English village. The Royal Signals installed generators, and the tents and messes and the hut that the Korean soldiers built for me were supplied with electricity. It was then possible to provide cinema shows for the officers and men. Just think of it, thousands of miles from home and loved ones, a stone's throw away from the menacing river, we could put on the latest films and provide once a week entertainment for all. This was greatly appreciated and helped to take away the inevitable boredom. The men were encouraged to make a little ground outside their tents attractive by growing flowers. I was placed in charge of the officers' mess garden, high up on a promontory, which overlooked the River Imjin.

My wife sent me a packet of seeds, which I planted in the landscaped garden. I called it Kew Gardens, and our regimental carpenter painted a sign bearing this ambitious name. To my great amusement the only things to appear after weeks of waiting and anticipation were just three dandelions.

When the church was finished an excellent notice board was placed outside, giving times of services and the events of the week. Curtains were fitted, making the church even more attractive and meaningful. I quote here an extract from *Japan News*.

In Korea recently, close by the River Imjin, a short and simple presentation of particular interest took place in St Martin's Church, the Regimental Church of 1st Commonwealth Divisional Signals Regiment. The service marked the 34th anniversary of the formation of the Royal Corps of Signals. During the past few months a close bond of friendship had developed between the Regiment, the men of whom were drawn from all parts of the United Kingdom, as well as from Canada, Australia, and New Zealand and the boys of Stratford Green County Secondary School in the County Borough of West Ham, London. It started through correspondence between Captain D. F. L. James, Royal Signals, of Forest Gate, London, serving with the Regiment, and his brother, M. B. G. James, who was the handicrafts master at the school. Mr James read portions of his brother's letter to the boys who showed such an interest in Far East current affairs that Captain James, beside writing interesting and vivid accounts of army life in Korea, sent descriptions of Korea, its people, their customs and history. The schoolboys soon identified themselves with the Regiment's welfare, and the church on the banks of the River Imjin. Captain James's letters reflected the pride of the Regiment in its church which started with a bare corrugated hut and was built up and improved entirely by the Regiment's efforts.

St. Martin's was a church which, although small, any parish or circuit could be proud. The boys of the school decided that their enthusiastic interest should take some practical form and so with the consent of Mr H. Munden, the headmaster, they fashioned in their woodwork and metal shops a carved oak cross and altar lantern. These were suitably engraved and sent to the Regiment and at a ceremony during a morning service were placed in the church. Captain James was chosen to make the presentation before a capacity congregation of men of the Regiment. He said: "I have been asked on behalf of the headmaster and boys of Stratford Green County

Secondary School in London, England, to accept the gift of a cross and lantern which were made by the boys, and to request the Commanding Officer to accept them for our Regimental church". Lieutenant-Colonel G. H. Starr in reply said: "I have great pleasure in accepting on behalf of the First Commonwealth Divisional Signal Regiment this cross and lantern. We are grateful to the headmaster and boys of Stratford Green School for these gifts which will enhance the beauty of the church. I will now ask our chaplain, Rev. Allan J. Bowers to dedicate them and place them on the altar. These gifts will remain in the church as a token of the admirable bond which from a small beginning has grown into a tangible and staunch friendship between the Royal Signals thousands of miles away in Korea and Stratford Green schoolboys in London.

27th July 1953 was a special day in Korea. It was the day when the war ended between North and South Korea, and the day that the armistice agreement between the United Nations and the Communists was signed at Panmunjum, not far from the regiment's position on the 38th Parallel. It was signed at 10 o'clock (2 a.m. British Summer Time) in a grimly silent ceremony that lasted only twelve minutes. Despite the solemnity of the occasion guns still boomed across the central zone and the smoke from explosions on the surrounding hills could be seen from the windows of the armistice hall, which had been finished after carpenters had worked all night in the rain to get it completed in time. Lieutenant-General William K. Harrison headed the United Nations contingent and sat at a table marked by a small United Nations flag, facing General Nam II, who sat at the North Korean-flagged table. He signed 36 copies of the agreement – 12 copies each in English, Korean, and Chinese. Despite that fact that the armistice had been agreed and all the documents signed, as night fell United Nations' troops set out into no-man's land and on their usual patrols. It was not until 10 o'clock that night that the battlefield fell silent as the cease-fire came into operation and soldiers unloaded their weapons, though they continued to carry ammunition with them. The cease-fire, like the signing ceremony, was strangely unemotional. There was no cheering or rejoicing and there was no celebration of the occasion, but profound thanks to God that the war was over. Some of us heard on the forces network General Mark Clark, United Nations Supreme Commander, say: "I cannot find it in me to exult in this hour, rather it is a time for prayer, that we may succeed in our difficult endeavour to turn this armistice to the advantage of mankind." At our church service on the following Sunday prayers of thanksgiving were said as we remembered all who had died in the war and all who had been injured, and special prayers were given as we remembered the families of all who were involved in the war. The men on the mountains from coast to coast, all the troops, like us in the First Divisional Signal Regiment, were profoundly relieved to know that at last there was peace.

There could be no sense of victory, for there were still a million Chinese in North Korea. The building in which the armistice agreement had been signed, a large structure built of bamboo wood and looking like a cross between a village hall and an eastern pagoda, was now silent and empty. Yet that morning, apart from the two opposing generals and their aides, 400 people had assembled there, half of whom were Communists who sat stiffly in segregated groups, the Chinese in drab uniform and the North Koreans, who looked far more military, wearing dark green jackets and dark blue trousers with red stripes. Those present will surely never forget that moment when, at 10 o'clock, General Harrison and General Nam II entered the hall from opposite doors, gave not the slightest sign of recognizing each other's presence, signed the necessary documents, and then rose and walked out.

I couldn't help but think as I sat in our church that the Western world had little knowledge of Korea before the Korean war was precipitated by the surprise attack from North Korea on 25th June 1950. The three-year war had brought untold suffering to the South Koreans, leaving almost the whole land devastated and more than a million killed or wounded in South Korea alone, not to forget men of the American forces, of whom 33,629 died, the Commonwealth Division, of whom 1,263 died, and those of other nations involved (Belgium, Columbia, Ethiopia, France, Greece, Holland, the Philippines, Thailand and Turkey), who between them lost 1,800 killed. In addition, many thousands of those who served in Korea were wounded.

As I mentioned earlier, Korea means: "Land of the morning calm"; it's a beautiful land and though I lived there for only a year, and my work as a chaplain took up most of my time, I had an opportunity of seeing the country and fell in love with it and its people.

Our officers' mess was built high on a promontory; it was a sheer delight to stand outside the mess when the moon was full, to look down upon the River Imjin and to see it shine in the soft moonlight, or in the morning to see the sun rise in all its splendour.

Korea was characterized by hills and mountains, which accounted for almost 80% of its territory. Low hills were predominant in the south and west, with higher mountains in the east and the north. Thus the western and southern slopes were gradual and met with the plains and winding river basins, while the eastern slopes plunged directly into the nearby East Sea. To the south was the Pacific Ocean. The peninsular area was about 86,500 square miles. Beaches were to be found where the streams emptied into the sea, which often took the

Officers' mess, Kew Gardens

form of coastal lagoons where the waters were clean and in peacetime attracted many holiday-makers.

Most of Korea's rivers flow into the Yellow Sea and the Pacific waters to the south after draining the gentler western and southern slopes of the peninsula. The rivers were important as a source of irrigation, and all water for drinking purposes was brought up from the River Imjin in water carts. More than 70% of Korea's rice fields depended on river water. It was only after the armistice was signed that it was possible to see the extent to which the country was ravaged by war with the armies that moved from Seoul to the tip of Pusan and most of the buildings destroyed and the hills stripped of

Allan before morning service

trees by people desperate for fuel. I was impressed to discover a variety of wild flowers, some of which I gathered on a Saturday afternoon to place on the altar for the Sunday morning early communion at 8 o'clock and the morning worship at 10 o'clock. Often I would stand for long periods looking at the mountains across the 38th Parallel, the dividing line between the north and south, and wondered if the two nations that had fought such terrible battles would ever become one nation. I was told that the aristocratic-looking heads of families would often go out into the countryside when the sun had set, just to think. I imagined that they had much to think about as they looked into the future and had a vision of a new Korea, a Korea where the welfare of all the people would be a first charge upon the government, together with the working out of a system of justice in all areas of national life and the bringing about of a spiritual reform by revamping the education system and developing higher cultural standards. I suspect that forward thinking Koreans will in due course challenge North Korea to accept a peaceful unification in the spirit of goodwill and mutual co-operation. I am sure that all who served in this far-off land would hope and pray that something good would come out of the war. It heartened me to know that Christianity was growing by the hour. I came across an old Korean proverb given to me by a Korean Christian in my Bible class: "Expect the unexpected and in the unexpected expect Christ". If there is to be a change in the right direction we can be sure that he who pitched his tent among us will be the way that change for the good will come about.

A special Sunday in August 1954 for our church was reported in the *Japan News* UK Section, as follows:

"1st Commonwealth Divisional Signals Regiment celebrate 3rd anniversary. Never before have men of the United Kingdom, Canada, Australia and New Zealand served together in an integrated Signal Regiment." These words formed part of a sermon preached by the Regimental Chaplain, Rev. Allan J. Bowers at a special service of thanksgiving, remembrance and re-dedication held on Sunday morning August 1st to mark the third anniversary of the formation of the

First Commonwealth Divisional Signal Regiment. The Regimental church of St Martin's was crowded with a representative Commonwealth congregation of worshippers. These included the General Officer Commanding, First Commonwealth Division, Major General H. Murray, CB, DSO, Brigadier T. T. Murdoch, OBE, Commander 28 Commonwealth Infantry Brigade, and Brigadier F. A. Clift, DSO, Commander 25th Canadian Infantry Brigade, and Brigadier J. T. Burrows, MA, Commander New Zealand "K" Force.

The lesson, Psalm 27, was read by General Murray. Commonwealth Signallers from every troop in the Regiment joined together with their Commanding Officer, Lt-Col G. H. Starr in giving thanks to God for the fine operational traditions and service of their integrated Regiment. The congregation also included representatives from the United States and ROK armies. The Regimental Chaplain took as his text, verse one of Psalm 133: "Behold how good and pleasant it is when brothers dwell together in unity". He commented, "If the Holy Bible was searched from cover to cover it would be difficult to find a more appropriate text to mark the occasion of the third anniversary of the formation of the First Commonwealth Divisional Signal Regiment which originally came into being on July 28th 1951. Unity has characterized its life, and the experience of all ranks concerned has been a good and pleasant one." Padre Bowers continued [by saying] he thought the Regiment has the spirit to ensure the highest possible standards both in work and play. The Latin motto: "Ubi Spiritus Ibi Libertas" was certainly true of this Regiment. The chaplain continued: "We in St Martin's Church, Korea, today thank God for the part the First Commonwealth Divisional Signal Regiment played during the fighting and trust God to bless its continued work during the truce."

Conditions of warfare in Korea presented many special problems of communications. The rugged terrain made wireless working difficult; poor roads and tracks which collapsed in time of flood made the dispatch riders' task truly hazardous. Static warfare resulted in a large build-up of cables with the consequent maintenance problems. The truce conditions offered the Signal Regiment another solid challenge: to build up the new static layout. Mobile training in 1954 meant adaptation to what was virtually a new role. All these hazards,

Padre Allan Bowers and the smallest manse in Methodism, built by the Koreans

tasks and challenges were successfully accepted and surmounted by the regiment.

Regimental welfare had achieved a high standard despite the unrelenting round-the-clock daily operating and maintenance of Divisional Communications, whether in war or in truce conditions. The First Commonwealth Divisional Signal Regiment represented the practical conception and success of a concerted Commonwealth effort. It had British and New Zealand troops together with some attached Australian Signal personnel. It faced the future with confidence and determination, sure and efficient in its manifold role and was quietly proud of its heritage.

Inevitably my year in Korea as a chaplain to the First Commonwealth Divisional Signal Regiment came to an end. It was an unforgettable year with memories deeply etched upon my mind. I felt privileged to have been chaplain to the First Commonwealth Divisional Signal Regiment and to have shared in the building of such a splendid church so near to the banks of the River Imjin.

Even though the armistice had been signed the armies of the North and South Koreans still faced each other and there was an uneasy peace. I hoped and prayed like many in the regiment that the war would not start up again.

My last day in the beautiful land was Sunday 8th August 1954, memorable in so far as I conducted my last service in the church. On this occasion the church was packed to the doors. It was the last time I heard the bells of St. Margaret's as they pealed out across the valley, calling men to worship.

One of the hymns we sang at the final service was: "Guide me, O Thou great Jehovah, pilgrim through this barren land". It truly was an emotional occasion to hear over one hundred men, many from Wales, sing this hymn. The land, ravaged by war, was in a sense barren, but there was much beauty to be seen everywhere.

Chapter Ten

England: Folkestone and Shornecliffe Garrison

My successor, The Reverend Wolsey Gilbert, from England, had only two days with me before I left for home. Later he wrote to me as follows:

Do you remember that I took over from you what surely must have been one of the smallest manses any Methodist minister has ever lived in, just one room, and you had it built for you by the Korean soldiers out of empty boxes and packing cases. I remember that it was built on a lovely hill after the war was over, overlooking the River Imjin. You called it, "The Hermitage". I must say that I was glad to see the back of you when you left Korea for England, and before there is any misunderstanding let me explain. You may remember that I travelled from Seoul with a New Zealand padre up to the First Divisional Signal Regiment. I think he was a Maori Prince. His name was Lawn Ikhu, well, at least that was the way it was pronounced. As he travelled he told me of a new epidemic that seemed to be sweeping the forces; it was haemorrhagic fever which was caused by termites that lived on the back of mice, and he warned me with due concern to stay clear of these little creatures Now, the first night I spent in the Regiment was in the visitor's tent. After a wash I clambered into my bed and put out the lamp. I tried to get some sleep but soon I was disturbed by something scratching on the sandbag walls, and when I flashed my torch, I saw two or three mice scampering around. Now I almost feel ashamed to mention it, but I was petrified. I had visions of myself getting this fever and dying within a week. It seems funny now but at the time I was scared stiff and didn't mention it to you or anyone else in the morning, but I can tell you now I was jolly glad when you moved out of your little hut so that I could move in.

Now, I dare say I forgot to say thank you for the running concern you left behind. I found it comparatively easy to pick up the work where you left it and I remember the lovely church, St Martin's in the Paddy. And I remember at the entrance was the old Korean bell that we used to ring calling the men to worship and the beautiful stained glass window set in the wall above the altar of the Madonna and Child which you had designed and made by an artist in the regiment. I also remember the choir practices that we used to have in the Sergeant's mess, when Ken Dawes, the doctor used to play the piano.

Sadly, within a few months after Wolsey had taken over from me, changes in the Divisional structure made it necessary for the church to be dismantled. The stained glass window was removed and taken back to England and placed in the Royal Signals Museum, Blandford Camp, Blandford Forum, Dorset. It marked the end of the life of this quite unique, wonderful building. I think of the many officers and men who worshipped in our church near the banks of the River Imjin who belonged to the Commonwealth and returned to their own countries. The church never ceased to be the church when the doors were closed, or even when they closed permanently. Few things kindle the fire of our religious faith more readily than Christians who talk glowingly about their Lord. I knew of three or four soldiers who entered the ministry of the church, and one officer, a spotter pilot during the Korean war, who became a missionary pilot in Africa; upon his return to England he went up and down the country playing gospel songs with his guitar and he told people about the love of Jesus.

As my jeep left the regiment I looked back and for the last time I saw the church we had built, St Martin's in the Paddy, and its pretty spire, so close to the River Imjin. The river was sparkling in the sunshine, winding like an enormous snake across the 38th Parallel. There was something unique about this church; it was a kind of symbol standing between North and South Korea, the spire pointing upward to the heavens, speaking silently of the way to end bellicosity between North and South, for God alone was the source of peace and the lover of concord. I wondered about the future of this wonderful country and people and whether the barrier between North and South would one day be taken down and the people become one.

As for the people of South Korea I came into contact with, I found them most charming, friendly and courteous. The country was very beautiful with its scenic landscapes, sheer waterfalls, fascinating caves, sandy beaches, rivers, a bird watcher's paradise. Though most of the country had become ruined by the war and its people devastated by grief through the loss of loved ones, I felt them to be so resourceful that in the course of a few years they would rebuild their land and become a new nation and people. There is a Korean poem, the author unknown, that aptly describes the steadfastness of nature as I witnessed it through the extreme heat of summer and the icy cold of winter, each season bringing a particular kind of beauty.

> The tree that strikes a deep root
> Is firm among the winds,
> Its flowers are good,
> Its fruit abundant.
>
> The stream whose source is deep
> Gushed forth even in drought.
> It forms a river
> And gains the sea.
>
> Let us live, let us live,
> Let us live in a green mountain.
> Eating wild grapes and vine berries,
> Let us live in a green mountain.

The journey down to Seoul on the main supply route covered me with white dust from the makeshift road used day and night to bring supplies to the front line. I boarded a plane at Seoul that took me to Inchon, a port facing the Yellow Sea, where I embarked on the *Empire Orwell*, the same troopship that had brought me out to Hong Kong in 1951. I couldn't stop thinking about those young men who came out with me on the troopship who were killed in the battles which took place in Korea; around one thousand, whose bodies lie in the United Nations' Cemetery in Pusan.

The journey back to England was extremely pleasurable. I had been separated from Betty for almost three years after only three weeks of marriage, and so there was an excitement in the prospect of meeting again. We had written every week during my stay overseas. I had arranged through a motorcar agent in Hong Kong to have a new car awaiting me at Southampton, where we were due to dock, and Betty had arranged to meet there. My absence from England seemed almost like a dream as the days and weeks seemed to drag by so slowly. Our meeting was wonderful indeed and in a short time we felt that we had never been apart. On our journey up to Richmond I was delighted to see the fields and meadows so green, such a contrast after living in places in the Far East close to rice paddy fields where there was no grass. Even to see the cows was a pleasure; all the time I was abroad we never had fresh milk!

We stayed in a hotel in Richmond, not far from our Theological Training College, before going to Folkestone where I was appointed as chaplain in the Folkestone and Shorncliffe Garrison, with special oversight of the Methodist Church in the seaside town of Sandgate, where soldiers in the garrison were invited to worship.

Our new army quarter was situated on Shorncliffe plain, where we had a lovely view of Folkestone Bay. This was our home for the next four years, and Jane, our beloved daughter, was born in the Military Hospital in Shorncliffe on the 13th August 1955. The telephone rang just after midnight and the army doctor told me that Betty had given birth to a baby daughter. Despite the late hour I rang my brother in Bristol and gave him the news. There is an old saying, "A son is a son till he takes a wife, but a daughter is a daughter for

Proud parents

the rest of her life". Jane brought us great joy. Grandma Bird, my mother-in-law, said she was as pretty as paint and she was.

The garrison was in being as long ago as the 1914–1918 war and some of the soldiers' quarters were those that had been used then. I remember my father telling me that at some time he had been stationed at Shorncliffe during the First World War. There were, of course modern quarters for the officers and men and a most beautiful garrison church. There was a well stocked NAAFI for service personnel and for wives and families. All the families were well looked after and there was a feeling of camaraderie in the garrison. I preached every Sunday morning in Sandgate Methodist Church and in the evenings preached in the Folkestone circuit, which often took

97

me into the heart of the Kent countryside. One of the chapels was situated at Stelling Minnis on the way to Canterbury, where stood the only remaining windmill in Kent. The Chapel Steward owned the windmill from which there was a breathtaking view of the Kent countryside. The old mill was still working and it was a joy to see the large blades turning in the wind. One Sunday we were saddened to see that one of the enormous blades was lying in the grass beside the mill. It had been blown off in a furious gale. I remarked to the steward, "I suppose the mill is no longer working." He replied with a chuckle in his voice and a smile on his weather-beaten face, "Of course she's working, even though temporarily handicapped." He called the windmill "The Queen of the Stars", because on a moonlit night the white windmill in the background of a dark sky reflected the brightness of the moon, and could be seen from all over the common. It has been remarked that materials, like people, are made interesting by their defects, and many visitors to Kent made a visit to see the windmill with one blade. Later it was turned into a museum, fully restored and open to the public.

Occasionally we went to Canterbury Cathedral to evensong. It was a joy to share in the service and hear the choir sing, their melodious voices filling the cathedral. We liked the old town of Canterbury with its ancient history. Sometimes we would visit Dover Castle on the way home to Folkestone. The white cliffs were fascinating to see, a reminder of the song the soldiers sang when our troopships approached the English coast after service overseas.

On the 26th of July 1956, when Jane was almost a year old, Colonel Nasser, the Egyptian dictator, nationalized the Suez Canal and I was told to hold myself in readiness to join a Casualty Clearing Station at Aldershot. Army reservists were called up and there were rumours of an all-out war with Egypt. Britain had been a principal shareholder in the company that controlled the canal. I said goodbye to Betty and our daughter as I was posted to Aldershot to join a team of doctors and two chaplains, an Anglican and a Roman Catholic. The Catholic chaplain was from Buckfast Abbey in Devon, and was responsible for designing stained glass church windows. We obtained tropical kit and were ready to move at a moment's notice.

The camp was full of jeeps, Land Rovers, and heavy vehicles painted in yellow. We carried out a casualty exercise and soldiers were given imaginary wounds, simulating those that are sustained in battle. The surgical operations were acted out by the doctors as we chaplains gave comfort to the wounded. What took place would be excellent for television drama but the senior doctor assured us that when we reached Suez it would be the real thing, though I had already seen shocking injuries in Korea.

Some of us felt that the Suez crisis was a "storm in a teacup", and would soon end. However, this was not the case. Anthony Eden, Prime Minister, ordered the bombing of Egyptian forces and sent troops to Port Said at the canal's northern end. Meanwhile, an advance party of the Casualty Clearing Station went out by plane to Suez. On the 31st of October France began hostilities by firing on an Egyptian destroyer. It seemed like the start of another world war. Early in the morning the 5th Airborne assault was launched on Port Said and Port Fuad by the British 3rd Parachute Battalion and the 16th Parachute Brigade. There was fierce fighting and some casualties. The Casualty Clearing Station had landed and was in action. Meanwhile, I went with the rear party to Southampton and embarked on the troopship *Empire Orwell*, which set sail on the evening tide for Port Said. On board there were hundreds of troops ready for action. We were well on our way to the Mediterranean when the ship's captain called the officers to his quarters near the bridge and told us that that the soldiers in Port Said had ceased action and been withdrawn under pressure from the United States and the United Nations without re-establishing control of the canal. The captain told us that the troopship would be sailing to Malta. This information was put out over the ship's broadcast system and a loud cheer went up from the troops. The war was over, and what a relief that was to all of us on board ship and especially to me when I thought of Betty and our daughter at Shorncliffe. How relieved Betty would be!

I went to bed that night and thanked God that it was over and I would soon be able to return home. I fell asleep, the throbbing engines as music to my soul. I remember waking the next morning and from my cabin window seeing a sunlit blue sky and the grand harbour of Valetta. The engines had stopped and the troopship tied up. The sun shone on the walls and buildings and the domes of the churches appeared as though a pot of gold had been poured over them. Everything was perfectly still and I recalled Wordsworth's poem:

Never did sun more beautifully steep
In his first splendour valley, rock, or hill;
Ne'er saw I, never felt, a calm so deep!

After disembarkation the men of the Casualty Clearing Station were accommodated in tents at Tuffietra Bay on the far side of the island. The island was truly beautiful as indicated in the Maltese National Anthem" "To this beautiful land, the mother that gave us our name". Though it was late November it was still very warm. We had Padres Hours and we went to the bay where St Paul was ship-wrecked. One of the soldiers came upon an old incendiary bomb sticking out of the red soil, a reminder of the heavy bombing the island endured during the war, for which it was awarded the George Cross for gallantry by the late King.

After an hour's climbing we saw in the distance St Paul's Bay; it was a small pear-shaped island, not far from the shore where we stood. On the island was a statue of St Paul and a small chapel. The soldiers gathered around me and I read the story of the shipwreck as told in a graphic way by St Luke in the Acts of the Apostles. On the way back to camp we saw the remains of the Roma Villa, which is said to have been the official residence of Publius, the chief man of the island and where Paul and Luke were received courteously and lodged for three days. In modern times the island has been called: "The Island of Sunshine and History". Its wonderful churches, with outstanding frescos and paintings, made this short visit memorable. Within a week of Christmas celebrations we left Luqa airport and landed at Southend-on-Sea, where we were taken by coach to London. I caught the evening train to Folkestone and arrived back at Shorncliffe camp where once again Betty and I were reunited, never to be separated again.

I continued my work in the garrison and with the help of some of the soldiers we made a beautiful chapel in the Sailors' and Soldiers' Home. A soldier helped design one of the large windows and made it a stained glass window depicting the call of St Paul on the road to Damascus. I conducted evening worship on Sundays and the building was also used as a recreation centre where soldiers could have refreshments.

One day I had to go to Aldershot camp and on the train I met an old soldier who was in the Battle of the Somme in the First World War, a battle widely regarded as one of the bloodiest and most controversial land battles ever to be fought. We soon got into conversation and he asked me if I would like to hear what had happened to him in the battle. I listened with rapt attention as he told me that he was among the first British troops to go over the top on 1st July 1916. He said that fifteen divisions of the army attacked north of the river. The German positions were strongly defended and rain had churned up the mud. It seemed that hundreds of soldiers were being mown down by heavy machine-gun fire. Shells were bursting dangerously near as he fell down and buried his face in the mud and dug in his hands in the terror of the moment. When the shelling ended and the dead were lying around him he relaxed, looked at the mud in his hand and saw something bright. He scraped the mud away and discovered it was a silver crucifix. How it came to be there he said only God knew but he felt that God had spoken to him direct from heaven in an answer to prayer. He said he looked at the crucifix and in doing so turned his thoughts to the scene of desolation outside the city wall where Jesus was crucified. He said he felt the wonderful peace of Christ and that his fears left him. He took from his pocket the silver crucifix and handed it to me to hold. He said that he had carried it with him wherever he went and that he had loved and served Christ who had come to him in that special way on the battlefield.

I read afterwards that on the first day of the Somme offensive 19,000 men of the British army had been killed in the greatest one day loss the army had ever known and that before the battle finally ended. four and a half months later in November 1916, a million soldiers of Britain, France and Germany had been killed. The old soldier whom I met on the train going to Aldershot was most fortunate in coming safely through the battle. The half-hour in which he gave me access to his mind and thoughts made me realize what a difference such a conversation had made for me. I pried into his mind and learned a great deal. Perhaps we should pry into each other's minds more than we do.

My six years as an army chaplain was soon to end. I came through the Hong Kong experience and the Korean war safely, though at times I was in grave danger. Life in the Folkstone and Shornecliffe Garrison was in effect a preparation for return to the civilian ministry. Betty and I were looking forward to it and especially to our invitation to the Leatherhead circuit in Surrey. However, it was not to be, for at the last moment the Stationing Committee changed the appointment to Grantham in Lincolnshire. By the first of September 1954 we were in Grantham to start our ministry in that town.

A week before leaving the army I received a letter from the Chaplain General, Canon Victor Pike. I remembered him saying in an address to us chaplains as we completed our course at Basgshot Park: "No man can be won for the king of God by argumentation", words originally spoken by William Temple. I had many lively discussions with soldiers in Padres' Hours, and even arguments, but I learned the truth of William Temple's words, which made it clear that much more was required than arguments. The letter read:

> Now that the time has come for your release from the army, please accept from me, on behalf of the Royal Army Chaplains' Department all best wishes for your future, which I trust will be greatly blessed by Almighty God. I hope you will take with you happy and encouraging memories of participation in a great team, whose service is to carry the Christian message to men and women under every circumstance and condition of life. We shall still remember you as you continue to serve God in other spheres, and ask a place in your prayers for the Royal Army Chaplains, for we all share in these days the high task of calling men and women to a realization of the Divine purpose. May God bless and strengthen you in all your ways, so that you may serve him faithfully in the ministry of his Church.

It was with some sadness that I left the Royal Army Chaplains' Department to return to the circuit ministry within Methodism, mainly because of the spirit of *esprit de corps* that I enjoyed with men and women of all ranks in the army, and the feeling of loyalty that one could count on among all ranks whether at home or abroad, and when in danger the feeling of comradeship and fellowship at deep levels.

I was asked more than once how I could reconcile being a chaplain in a service that at any time could be engaged in warfare and possible killing. I never had a problem with this question for I believed that soldiers, just as much as civilians, needed spiritual oversight to live a life as fully as one was able in tune with the Spirit of Christ through grace and faith. At no time would any chaplain be required to engage in fighting, and in this respect received protection under the Geneva Convention.

We looked forward very much to the new appointment after leaving the army, but we loved army life and there were adjustments to be made, so we wondered just how we would find the new experience, working together in the civilian ministry.

Chapter Eleven

Grantham

Changing from army life to the civilian ministry didn't worry me over much. The Superintendent minister of the Grantham circuit was an ex RAF chaplain, and so we had many things in common. Starting afresh after six years in the army I asked myself the question: what do people look for in their new minister? Some will look to the minister to fill the church, and if he does they will rate his ministry a success. But others, may their number increase, will help their pastor to bring people within and without the walls of the church to a knowledge of the transforming friendship of Christ.

He will be expected to be a good preacher, though some ministers and the laity question preaching as a means of communicating. I think the late Bishop of Lichfield, Dr E. Wood, right in what he wrote: "Preaching with meticulous care, based on deep thought and wide reading, and charged with the power won in the secret place of prayer is not mere utterance, it is powerful to change the hearts of men, and indirectly but very really, to affect the course of history". The task of preaching has never been easy, but as Dr D. Martyn Lloyd-Jones has written: "The work of preaching is the highest and greatest and the most glorious calling to which anyone can ever be called".

Some will expect the minister to visit them in their homes. I am idealistic enough to believe that pastoral visitation is an important part of our work as ministers. But it should be a shared responsibility with the laity, and to save valuable time visitation should be by prior arrangement.

It will be expected that he is a good administrator. The congregation has a right to expect this, for a church cannot be successfully run unless it has efficient administration. He will also need to be a teacher, but he must never forget Paul's words to Timothy: "Take heed to yourself and to your teaching", so he will be expected first and always first to be a man of prayer, one who knows his Bible, one who is filled with the Spirit of Christ. Who is sufficient for these things? If he rises to these expectations, it will not be entirely due to his own efforts; it will be because he has received freely of God's grace and been encouraged by the prayers of his people.

What will be expected of the minister's wife? If his wife has a job to go to she will not be able to take her place at the Women's Meeting on a weekday afternoon, or attend the coffee mornings or sales of work, and if she has a young family, it will be equally difficult to be in the centre of things. "Alas," some will say, "parsons' wives are not what they used to be."

Some time ago a parson's wife wrote about the lousy job of being a parson's wife in an article in a national newspaper entitled, "Never marry a Cleric". She was disillusioned. She wrote:

I had visions of entering with my husband into the great work of converting the world (who doesn't at twenty-one), but here I am surrounded by four children tied to the home, expected to turn up at every function, and feeling like a widow as my husband is always on duty. Surely Jesus wants a nurse where she is needed, rather than a do-gooder, where she is not needed. Serving ought not to mean raising money for a carpet down the aisle, but it so often does. The Church seems so far away from the ideals of youth and the teachings of Jesus.

Times have changed, working wives have come to stay, old ways of ministry are giving place to new, but the gospel is everlasting and does not change. It is always a spoken message and what that message says. The verbs used with it are always those like "announce", "proclaim", "speak", or "receive", "hear", "obey" The minister who ministers is one who is active, ideally with his wife, in the church or churches to which he is appointed. But what is important is for the minister, his wife, family and congregation to accept one another. "In a word, accept one another as Christ accepted us, to the glory of God" (New English Bible, Romans 15.7), to realize each other's limitations, but to share each other's visions and dreams and work together for a more relevant church. With these thoughts I began my ministry in Grantham in September 1957.

The little town of Grantham in Lincolnshire was noted for its parish church of St Wulfram with its soaring 282 ft spire, which we could see from our manse front door, one of the most important town churches in England. In the town stood the imposing bronze statue of Sir Isaac Newton, who was a famous pupil of Grantham's King's School.

Soon after we arrived in Grantham we met Margaret Thatcher's mother and father, who worshipped regularly in the town's Methodist Church, situated in Finkin Street, where I preached from time to time. Alfred Roberts, her father, was a Local Preacher in the circuit. Margaret had her father's good looks and acknowledged when she became Prime Minister that she owed almost everything to him. This was, I suspect, an overstatement, for her mother taught her from birth the rights and wrongs of conduct. However, when Margaret became famous she managed to exclude all references to her mother, Beatrice Roberts.

I remember the grocery shop at the crossroads of the A1 and the road to Nottingham, and meeting Alfred and Beatrice Roberts during my pastoral visits. When he worked in the shop he wore a white jacket and hat. It fascinated me to see him making pats of butter from a large block, and doing it so quickly.

Alfred was a self-made man who possessed a string of Victorian values. He was Mayor of Grantham in 1945, when he worked tirelessly for the town. I was privileged to know him and to enjoy his fellowship and occasional preaching. After Beatrice died he had fellowship with us in our manse when he came for an evening meal. He was proud of his two daughters and delighted in showing us their photographs. It was, however, noticeable that it was Margaret and not Muriel, the other daughter, that he talked about most. During the time we lived in Grantham Margaret had only just begun her life in politics.

Working in the Grantham circuit gave me a taste again of rural Methodism. Finkin Street was the head of the circuit. There were three other churches in the town, Harrowby Road, on a new estate area, looked after by Sister Olive Greensmith, a deeply committed deaconess who extended the hand of friendship, Commercial Road, looked after by Douglas Westington, a good friend, and Wesley on the other side of the town, for which I was responsible and which, despite the valiant efforts of a small band of people, had to close.

During my stay in Grantham I met a second-hand dealer called Johnny Wallwork, who had a large selection of antiques and well-worn furniture the like of which could be seen in many second-hand shops up and down the country. I did, however, obtain from him an oil painting by Sir David Cameron for three shillings that later I took to Christie's in London and sold for £180.

Douglas Westington was a splendid colleague and was also a real friend. On the day we moved into our manse he came and helped unload my library books. I discovered that we had both attended the Southbourne Methodist Church, Bournemouth, and though we never met then, we attended the same Bible Class, run by a Mr Boocock, whose Christian example and leadership meant so much to us in the early days of the war. Being appointed to the Grantham circuit was the one and only time that Conference changed my appointment. I never regretted it, and though we only stayed four years it was an excellent learning appointment for the rest of my ministry.

During this time I joined the Institute of Religion and Medicine, and continued my interest in those subjects. I would like to have trained as a doctor, thus combining my calling with medicine, and to have gone overseas to a missionary station. My interest in medical matters began in the RAF, where I worked on medical statistics at Air Ministry in Ruislip, Middlesex. I was particularly interested in medical ethics and the problems of medical care that arose around advances in knowledge and skill. Artificial insemination in some cases of childlessness represented a new remedy for barren marriages, but it also raised difficult questions about the nature of parenthood and relationship, and so, too, with contraception, especially the pill, which in many cases encouraged free sex. Alongside this were the questions of euthanasia, organ transplants, and the right to tell the patient. And so medicine and religion, which have always been associated, came in closer contact and prompted my interest in the healing ministry that later was further developed in healing services.

In the Grantham days the healing ministry was a sensitive subject. It was not a new thing in the church as there was plenty of evidence of the healing ministry of Jesus and others in the New Testament. Dr Leslie Weatherhead was a protagonist in the ministry of healing, and practised it in co-operation with doctors at the City Temple in London. His book: *Psychology, Religion and Healing*, his magnum opus, gained him a PhD at London University. Through Leslie Weatherhead's book I was introduced to the work of C. G. Jung, the Swiss psychiatrist, founder of "Analytic Psychology", an original thinker who made an immense contribution to the understanding of the human mind.

Every clergyman and clergywoman has met people whose deep-rooted problem was locked up with mind over matter, so essential for the health of body and mind. Thus, Professor Jung wrote:

> Among all my patients in the second half of life, that is to say, over thirty five, there has been no one whose problem in the last resort was not that of finding a religious outlook on life. It is safe to say that every one of them fell ill because he had lost that which the living religions of every age have given to their followers, and none of them has been really healed who did not regain his religious outlook.
>
> (Jung, *Modern Man in Search of a Soul*, 1933, p. 264)

I firmly believe this, and although at this stage I did not hold healing services, I frequently laid hands upon the sick when visiting people's homes or the hospitals. It was in those days that the greetings card industry had the idea of "Get well cards", which caught on and seemed to have a strong psychological effect upon those who had become ill for one reason or another.

Just three miles from Grantham was Belton House, set in 1,300 acres of deer park, an historic house attracting many thousands of visitors each year. In a visit to Belton House I was interested to see a chapel in the centre of the house, and reflecting upon this made me realize how important it is for every Christian home to have a place for being alone with God, for saying prayers and developing the spiritual life. Indeed at this time House Churches were springing up as offshoots of fixed places of worship, not unlike the church in the house of the first century, described in the charming letter of Philemon in the New Testament.

One can expect the unexpected in churches in and around Grantham, such as the chained library at St Wulfram's Church in Grantham, and the wall paintings at Corby Glen, where I also had pastoral charge of the Methodist Church.

Woolsthorpe Manor was the place where Sir Isaac Newton was born in 1642, a farmhouse just seven miles from Grantham. I mention these various places of interest because Betty and I had much joy in visiting them and improving our knowledge of their history.

It was while in Grantham, a strictly agricultural town, that we entered upon the egg industry. My father-in-law, Harry Bird, a farmer in Derbyshire, kindly supplied us with six hens. We had a large garden and I built a suitable pen for these hens. For weeks I went every day to see if they had laid any eggs but nothing happened. One day I was filled with excitement as I carried two brown eggs to show Betty. Thereafter we had eggs galore, so many that we could give some away and others we had to send to the packing station.

Rural Methodism was a challenge to me and it was a joy to minister to country folk in the small chapels spread over the Lincolnshire countryside. I learned a great deal from my stay in Lincolnshire. Our four years in Grantham came to an end and I accepted an invitation to go to Sheffield, mainly on the suggestion of our friend Dr Leslie Ward Kay, Vice President of the Conference at Birmingham in 1953, when Donald Soper was President. I was to be minister of Hillsborough Trinity Methodist Church, a church that overlooked Hillsborough Park and was within a stone's throw of Hillsborough football ground. This appointment was to open new fields of ministry in the city of steel and widen my experience of human nature.

As we moved from circuit to circuit the text "I will go in the strength of the Lord" helped me greatly, especially the power of this verse, when in September 1961 we occupied a manse in Overton Road. Our daughter Jane was six, and as the manse was very large she was full of excitement as she ran up and down the passages looking in each of the rooms and exclaiming: "Ooh mummy!"

I had pastoral charge of three churches, Hillsborough Trinity, my main church, Parkwood Springs, not true to its name as it was in the centre of the city not far from a gasometer, and Scotland Street, an old church. It has often been said that a minister has to be a "Jack of all trades" and when we moved to Sheffield, I wrote the following, with apologies to W. S. Gilbert.

I am the very model of the modern circuit minister.
My versatile efficiency seems positively sinister,
With youth I'm awfully jolly, and with older folks refined.
I'm a staunch denominationalist, yet ecumenically inclined.
I'm very much au fait in matters modern theological.
The "myths" of Genesis I correlate with dogmas geological.
I'm chummy with the Rotary, and with women's groups the same.
I present the social gospel in a way that brings no shame.
I polish resolutions up for all assemblies solemn,
And for the monthly newsletter write a pastoral bright column.
I can publicize a triumph and soft pedal a disaster.
I'm the very model of the dynamic modern pastor.
I'm up to date in culture; about art I wax rhapsodical.
In church administration I'm fantastically methodical.
I'm very good at counselling and I preach a snappy sermon;
And stewardship potentials I can skilfully determine.
I'm learned in liturgies and I'm ceremonially adept,
Yet the bounds of taste and safety I have never overstepped.
My versatile efficiency is positively sinister,
I am the very model of the modern circuit minister.

Chapter Twelve

Sheffield

Sheffield was known as the city of steel. There were many steel works and lots of individual factories where some of the finest cutlery was made. I recall visiting one of my members who occupied a flat over the steel works. It was while she was in the kitchen making a cup of tea that the hammers in the factory started operating. Everything on the mantelpiece seemed to move and the noise was deafening. I asked how she could live with the noise and vibration and she replied, "After forty years one gets used to it!"

We found the people of Sheffield very friendly and most generous. There was a fish and chip shop at the bottom of our road and the first time I went in for fish and chips the lady owner, who saw I was wearing a clerical collar, said that there was no charge. She had a special place in her heart for parsons, but next time I insisted on paying. The chemist only charged half price and when I paid him the money he said it was half price because of what parsons did for suffering humanity. The dentist never charged and the optician did our eye tests and glasses free. I have never seen such kindness and generosity as we received in Sheffield.

Our church overlooked Hillsborough Park. It was a splendid building and even had its own billiard room with two full size billiard tables. Among the members was a millionairess who gave each minister of the church an extra three pounds a week to his stipend and two days before Christmas her chauffeur brought an eleven pound turkey. She was a member of the Wigfall family, which had many shops in the Midlands supplying television sets and kitchen and household goods. Her father, Henry Wigfall, started the business by going round Sheffield selling wares on a bicycle. This lady was a Methodist through and through, and gave much money to the church.

We had a splendid drama group led by Mr Roy Wain. We became good friends but I had to put my foot down when he and I had a difference of opinion about the language used in a play and a punchbowl of intoxicating liquor that was to appear on the stage. Methodism in those days was very strict about the right use of premises and we were governed by unalterable rules. There happened to be a journalist in the play and my refusal to allow it to go on stage without the necessary alteration was reported to a news agency and the matter appeared in all the national newspapers. I had a great number of letters approving my stand, and the leader of the drama group gave me all scripts to read for future plays. We remained very good friends.

It was said by one of the down-to-earth Yorkshire people that when I came to Sheffield I seemed to lack a sense of humour, but after a few months of dealing with these honest men and women I became one of them. The gentleman in question reminded me long after I had left Sheffield that at a Leaders' meeting when we discussed who would open the new hall, I had said that I would arrange to meet him at his convenience, and I couldn't understand why they all laughed.

Our experience at Sheffield of adding new buildings to the sets of church premises began with a large extension to the church hall, costing some thousands of pounds. The architect was a member of the Congregational Church; he was getting on in years and always began his conversation on the telephone with "Are you there?" I had to smile because I had so often heard people say about God "Are you there?"

I met Jack Pike, Senior Steward, who gave me confidence, in our Hillsborough church. He said to me one day, "Allan, you can turn things round on a sixpence!" I doubt if he knew what help this gave me through the years, especially embarking on church building schemes.

While at Sheffield I became the District Chapel Secretary and worked closely with the District Chairman, George Percival, a lovely, affable man, known for his cheerful spirit and fund of stories. I had reason to thank God for my early training in a lawyer's office when dealing with large schemes for church buildings involving thousands of pounds.

I referred earlier to the need for a sense of humour. All ministers will know what a valuable asset humour is, and we all know how it can ease the burdens of life and deepen fellowship and even reveal human frailty. I often saw the funny side of things. Soon after we arrived at the manse at Sheffield a small man arrived at the back door carrying a black case. With little thought I remarked, "You must be the gas man to read the meter!", whereupon he replied, "No, I'm not the gas man, I'm the doctor!" We had a good laugh and from that moment we became firm friends. On one occasion he judged the crowning of the queen in our church and, despite the fact that he was an orthodox Jew, he joined in the event with obvious pleasure. Tragically, he and his wife were killed in an aircraft disaster on their way to spend a holiday abroad.

I always believed pastoral visitation to be high on the ministers' priorities. The need for this had been stressed in college by Reverend Dr John T. Wilkinson, who lectured on "Pastoralia" and introduced us to a splendid book, *The Reformed Pastor* (1665), by Richard Baxter, based on the Acts of the Apostles 20, verse 28: "Take heed therefore to yourselves, and to all the flock over which the Holy Ghost hath made you overseers, to feed the Church of God, which he hath purchased with his own blood". It was my concern for the care of "all the flock" that prompted me to introduce to the church "The Watchman Scheme", where members were appointed with responsibility for the oversight of other members and adherents, to keep in touch with them and to meet them from time to time to build each other up in the Christian faith. It worked well in my Sheffield church and was still in being many years after when I visited the church during an anniversary celebration.

A great deal of my time in the ministry seems to have been taken up with building schemes. My first was the new hall at Hillsborough Trinity, which opened on Saturday 16th November 1963 and included a splendid stage for drama, a new kitchen and ancillary rooms. We had to raise the sum of £12,000, which at that time was an enormous sum of money, but through the enthusiasm of the members and friends the money was raised. Betty and I daringly opened a shop on the premises to raise money. We opened three times a week and sold most things a housewife would need. It was then that I discovered the truth of a remark made by Mr McLeod, the Shadow Chancellor: "Money is the root of all progress".

During our ministry in Sheffield we led a party to the Holy Land, which was unforgettable. Reading the Bible became a new experience from that time onward. Unfortunately we had to leave the Holy Land earlier than planned because of the start of the Six Day War. We had to charter a special plane to bring us home. We heard machine-gun fire at night during our short stay at a hotel in Nazareth. It was a frightening experience and cast a shadow over the holiday. However, we managed to cross the Lake Sea of Galilee and to visit Capernaum and take Holy Communion in a charming chapel by the lake near where the feeding of the five thousand took place.

I will always be grateful that I had a ministry in Sheffield, for the people I met there, for their warmth, friendship and generosity. I also was privileged to join in philosophy seminars at the university and in the cut and thrust of discussion at those seminars to expand my understanding of philosophy. to look at faith in some depth, and search for a rational and clear articulation of the things I believed.

One day as I left the university I came across a second-hand shop in a back street. In the window, among a lot of junk, was a portrait of John Wesley, an oil painting that at first glance I thought was original. I paid £2.10 shillings (£2.50) for it and today it is valued at more than £5,000. I had the painting cleaned and asked Mr Peter Forsaith, of Westminster College, Oxford, knowledgeable on the Wesley portraits, to examine it. In his report he said it was undoubtedly a painting of John Wesley and since it did not relate to any other painting it would point to the fact of being taken "from life". From

Reverend John Wesley, M.A.

what he had seen of other work he thought it could have been painted in the 18th century, and the quality of the painting, especially the eyes, suggested a painter of some ability. Unfortunately, the signature couldn't be seen on the painting. From Wesley's journal it is clear that he had his portrait painted several times. For example, on December 22nd 1787, he wrote: "I yielded to the importunity of a painter, and sat an hour and a half in all for my picture. I think it was the best that was ever taken". Among other painters of Wesley's portrait was Sir Joshua Reynolds, but this has been lost. Could it be that the portrait I proudly possessed, found in the old junk shop, was painted by Sir Joshua Reynolds, RA? If so, it would be of much greater value than I am told it is worth. However, the value of this painting was not in money terms but in having an original portrait of the founder of Methodism, one of the greatest Christians of his age.

While in Sheffield I decided to keep a day-by-day diary of my activities. For forty years I have done this, totalling more than three million words so far. The idea was given to me at college by the tutor in Church History, who suggested that we students begin with "A Commonplace Book", putting down thoughts and ideas with particular reference to church life. From my Commonplace Book there developed a daily diary. After forty years I ask myself, as Virginia Woolf once asked, "I wonder why I do it?" But I found it most useful when trying to recall past events. I also found it useful as a preaching diary, recording each service taken, and sermon preached.

My diary, or journal, serves as a kind of looking glass, seeing my inner face, my deeper feelings, and my general state of health, physically and spiritually, which, like the daily weather I record, changed from day to day. I also enjoy writing about events of special interest that in retrospect can be read with joy. Without a diary everything soon went into oblivion, without recall from my deeper unconscious where it stayed buried. One can record the secret history of one's heart and conduct and even record secret faults that only God, "from whom no secrets are hid", is privy to. John Wesley, founder of Methodism, kept a journal over many years that provides fascinating readings and insights into his relationship with God and showed how he developed spiritually. In reading his journal I felt myself to be in the presence of a finely-tuned soul, never dull and always readable. It would be impossible to match such a person's skill at writing a journal, but it does at least encourage me in life's endeavour to live a godly life and develop religious strengths and insights. By reading such "journals of conscience" as those of John Wesley, Samuel Pepys, John Bunyan, and Virginia Woolf, I glimpsed the meaning of life. My diaries, some twenty-five or more large box files, stand on shelves in my garage. I have tried, upon Dr Johnson's recommendation, to keep them honestly. They give the life of a Methodist minister over forty years. Alas, I should have started when I began my active ministry in the Matlock Trinity circuit in 1946.

In some ways the most formative years of my ministry were these six years I spent in Sheffield. I learned much in the study of philosophy and enjoyed the challenge and inspiration when attending philosophy seminars at the University of Sheffield. I was also determined to make a daily study in the rigorous, relevant study of the Bible, for the sake of preaching and also to prepare my studies for a Batchelor's Degree in Divinity at the University of London.

Chapter Thirteen

Bebington

We left Sheffield in August 1967 to go to the Bebington circuit in the Wirral. I recall visiting the Circuit Steward in February 1965, one Saturday morning, with Betty and Jane. In those days it was usual for a minister to have his appointment fixed two years in advance. As soon as we were introduced we all got into a car for a tour of the circuit. Our first port of call was the Bridge Inn in the village of Port Sunlight, where we had lunch. Sitting at another table was the Conservative member of parliament for Bebington, the Rt Hon Geoffrey Howe. There were eight churches in the circuit and I was to have responsibility for Lower Bebington and Higher Bebington churches. I gladly accepted the invitation and joined the circuit at the close of our Sheffield ministry in 1967.

The members of the staff were particularly interesting, Dr Denis Inman, a splendid preacher and scholar, David Tripp, later to become Dr David Tripp, who transferred to the American Methodist Church and was also a scholar and author, and Sister Gwen Appleton a deaconess. It was a happy staff and every year we went to the theatre in Liverpool, with Betty providing a delicious supper afterwards. Writing about these occasions Denis put it as follows:

> One year I recall we saw Bernard Shaw's *Mrs. Warren's Profession* but such was your misgiving, Allan, that significantly the next year

we saw a Greek play and moved into a higher cultural level. Just as much a highlight of those evenings was what came by way of afters, back to the manse at Lower Bebington to a table laden with goodies, that matched, I am sure, anything that you had as a family in the United States of America.

I will always be grateful to David, who wrote a scholarly book, *Renewal of the Covenant*, published by Epworth Press, 1969, and for his massive knowledge of the early Church Fathers, some of which he imparted to me when he lectured at a ministerial training conference.

Sister Gwen was a friendly soul and we worked well together. On one occasion I had to go out to one of her churches to take a wedding as she was not an "authorized person". The church was full and the bridegroom with his best man came into the vestry before the ceremony. I asked Sister Gwen for the Registrar's certificate, the authority for me to perform the marriage, whereupon she told me that she hadn't got it. I said I couldn't perform the marriage without it. It seemed that I would have to make an announcement to the waiting congregation and inform them that the marriage could not take place on that day. However, giving it further thought and in order to avoid a difficult and embarrassing situation and disappointment for everyone, I informed the bridegroom and the best man that I would allow the marriage ceremony to take place, but that the bride and bridegroom would have to come back on the following Wednesday with a special licence, when I could go through the ceremony again privately and issue the appropriate certificate so that then they could sign the registers legally and all would be in perfect order. This we did on the following Wednesday and since they were married by the church on the first occasion, though not legally, they were not "living in sin". The congregation was none the wiser and the happy occasion went ahead without any problem. The Registrar told me I had done the correct thing. It would have been illegal if the registers had been signed without the appropriate certificate, and as the authorized person, I may have had my authorization taken away for future marriages.

At the next wedding I had with Sister Gwen the bridesmaid fainted, and we had to revive her before the ceremony could take place. Sister Gwen thought she had a jinx on weddings. We both laughed about it and for good measure at the next wedding the bride didn't turn up on time and the organist, who knew only one tune appropriate to a wedding, played "I'll walk beside you" for half an hour. It turned out that the bride's car had turned up late to collect her. These are but a few of the tribulations that a minister may experience when conducting weddings.

July 21st 1969 will always be regarded as a "Red Letter Day", for this was the day when, for the first time in history, a man landed on the moon. The old saying: "Cry for the moon", meaning to want the impossible, was outmoded. I record it only because, with excitement and bated breath, the whole world watched Armstrong and Aldrin guide the spacecraft gently down over the surface of the Sea of Tranquility and, with a hop to clear a crater the size of a football pitch, dropped smoothly to the surface.

During our stay in Lower Bebington an exchange of pastorates was arranged and we were appointed to go to a Methodist Church in the city of Eugene in the American state of Oregon for six weeks. We were exchanging pastorates with the Reverend Andrews and his family. It was the summer of 1971. After many goodbyes from friends of the church at Bebington we left for Manchester airport and boarded the BOAC plane for New York. A dear friend, Watson Thomas, waved farewell to us as the plane took off and he drove our car back to Bebington.

Chapter Fourteen

America

The sky was cloudy but within minutes the jet had climbed above the clouds and was bathed in sunshine, and I thought of the poet's words: "Wither O Splendid ship, wither away fair rover, and what thy quest?"

We had a good flight and as we approached New York the captain told us that we would be flying over the Empire State Building before landing at Kennedy airport. Our first glimpse of New York was a sea of skyscrapers, and as we began to lose height we had an amazing view of a network of roads carrying New Yorkers in and out of the great city, and finally we landed at Kennedy airport, a vast terminal covering over 600 square acres. In the arrivals area the administration desks of many countries' airlines formed one tremendous circle.

At customs we were greeted by an American official who smiled warmly and said, "Hi folks, welcome to America."

When we left the airport, which was air-conditioned, the heat of New York made itself felt with vengeance. After spending the night at a Holiday Inn Hotel on the perimeter of the airport we boarded a United Airlines jet bound for Chicago. At Chicago we met a heat wave, the temperature being in the nineties! The taxi cab driver, his face like black ebony and shining as if it had been polished, replied to Betty, who remarked about the heat while wiping away the perspiration from her face, "This ain't hot ma'am, dis is only cool."! He told us that Chicago was the second largest city in the United States, having a population of three and a half million and a metropolitan area containing over six million people.

We felt a strong wind blowing from Lake Michigan, which was why the city was called "the Windy City". We stayed the night at a Holiday Inn Hotel and had the luxury of air-conditioning in our bedroom, a shower unit and a bathroom, and colour television. I took a swim in the open-air swimming pool while Betty and Jane were getting ready for the evening meal.

We were impressed by the hygiene in the American hotels. The drinking glasses were sealed in polythene bags and the toilets were spotlessly clean, with disposable polythene covering on the seats.

The next day saw us on the last stretch of the five thousand mile journey to Eugene in Oregon. We flew over six states, Illinois, Iowa, South Dakota, Montana, Idaho and finally Oregon, having crossed the Rivers Mississippi and Missouri and the Rocky Mountains. Before landing at Portland we saw the snow-capped Mount Hood, 11,235 feet high, the heavily wooded forests and the Columbia River bounded by its farming communities, villages and towns.

Portland appeared to be a beautiful city and we had time to look around the gardens near the airport. At 7.20 p.m. we were met by the Williams family, Jerold and Janet, Bobby, Ruth, and baby Wendy. We were driven in their large station wagon one hundred and twenty miles down the freeway into Eugene, arriving at the parsonage in complete darkness at 10.30 p.m. I can tell you that we needed no rocking that night.

"The parsonage", as it was called in America, was a large bungalow-type building, very comfortable and airy. The kitchen had a wonderful deep freezer and fridge and the Williamses, through the arrangements committee, had filled both with food. Everything in the kitchen was modern, a housewife's dream, and there was a garbage disposal unit that was quite a new gadget for us. Just off the kitchen was another room with a washing machine, dishwasher, and drying machine.

The large garden had automatic sprinklers and was called "the back yard". It was beautifully landscaped and there was a rose garden full of a variety of roses. Everything we saw in the house and around seemed to be on a large scale; the robins were twice the size of ours at home and in the parsonage was an enormous cat with a fluffy white coat. We were told that he had to be fed on liver, sausage, and condensed milk. There were three goldfish in a large bowl but unfortunately they died while we were in residence, much to our concern.

From the large window we had a view of the Coburg hills. We were living in what was known as "millionaire's row". All the residences were extensive and had swimming pools.

Wesley United Methodist Church, set at the side of the parsonage, was in two acres of ground, with a spacious car park and offices. I had my own office and secretary, who was responsible for running the administration of the church. The church was an offshoot of the First Methodist Church, Eugene, which was started by a handful of people seventeen years ago. The parsonage was built first, then the fellowship hall with its ancillary classrooms and offices. The church, with its slanted roof, was dominated by three tall wooden crosses, symbolizing the sovereignty of Christ and the victory of good over evil.

The services on Sunday during our stay were held at 9.30 a.m., the only service of the day. Young people wearing labels with their Christian names displayed stood at the entrance to greet worshippers, and ushers showed them to their seats. Acolytes, dressed in black gowns with white silk collars, walked with dignity up the central aisle as the organ played the prelude, and after lighting the tall candles on the marble-topped communion table, they returned to their places. Jane was invited to do this during our stay and I was proud to follow her up the aisle to the communion table where on one side was the American Flag and on the other the Union Jack. The lay leader then processed with the minister to the pulpit and then went to the lectern to conduct the service. The order of service was printed for each Sunday. When the gowned choir did not sing an anthem a soloist sang. During the service each member of the congregation was invited to fill in a registration card, giving their name and address and, if they wished, any remarks about the sermon. These were handed to the church secretary who, on the following day, sent a welcome letter informing them that the minister would visit them as soon as possible. After each service members of the congregation were invited into the hall for coffee, tea or iced drinks, served with cookies. As a visiting minister I found this most helpful in getting to know members of the congregation.

After our first Sunday morning service, which was the 4th of July 1971, Independence Day, we went for a barbecue meal in the garden of one of the members and later that day we went to the Oregon university stadium and watched a magnificent display of fireworks. Our second Sunday at the church was the Charter Day Service, and at 1 o'clock about 130 people gathered for a barbecue chicken lunch, which was served at decorated tables in the church grounds with a variety of salads, cheese and pineapple, hot beans, vegetables, and fruit salad. After this gorgeous spread there was a large range of desserts, cherry pie, banana pie, blueberry pie, pumpkin pie, and lots of cakes topped with cream and chocolate. We sat down at tables in the warm sunshine and thoroughly enjoyed the meal. As I sat with Betty and Jane the thought came to me, "All this and heaven too".

Eugene was a beautiful city, founded in 1866 by Eugene Skinner, the first white settler. It lay in a lovely valley, through which flowed the Willamette and Mackenzie Rivers. Eugene covered twenty-eight square miles and had a population of 70,000. The shops and shopping centres were modern and beautifully laid out. In the centre were adventure playgrounds to amuse the children while their parents went shopping. The city hall was a modern building surrounded by water and fountains.

One afternoon I was invited to meet the mayor of Eugene in the city hall. We had a profitable discussion, which I recorded, and it included a message for the mayor of Bebington.

Every Saturday morning, outside the city hall "hippies" were allowed to hold a market, the only condition being that everything sold had to be hand-made. All the hippies I saw were clean; some belonged to the growing Jesus movement and I noticed that some of them wore wooden crosses round their necks. Every stall had coloured candles. Americans loved to have lighted candles at family meals.

During our six weeks' ministry I had two weddings, but before I could conduct the ceremony I had to register at the courthouse. Registration cost me $1.70 but ever after I could marry anyone in Oregon. Before a marriage licence was issued a blood test had to be undergone by the bride and bridegroom. When the certificate was issued the minister could marry the couple in the church, in their own garden, or even among the rhododendron bushes!

In the church there was a bridal room, exclusively furnished for the use of the bride and used before the ceremony as her dressing room. The reception was provided by the church for a fee of $55, and held in the fellowship hall. Guests were received by the bride and bridegroom and matron of honour. There were no speeches but a large cake was provided with tea, coffee, or iced punch. As each guest went into the hall they were invited to sign a guest book and handed a small bag of rice neatly tied in muslin, together with a scroll tied in a mauve ribbon with a verse from St Paul's hymn of love, and containing the words: "Thank you for sharing with us in the precious moments of this memorable day", and the names of the bride and bridegroom were added.

I had to conduct two funerals during our stay in Eugene and, sadly, one of the funerals was of a soldier killed in Vietnam. His body was brought back to America and he was buried with full military honours. After the committal and the firing of a volley of shots the American flag that had been removed from the coffin was folded with great dignity and handed by an officer in charge of the funeral to the parents, who were seated around the open grave. The officer handing the flag to the parents said: "I present this flag to you on behalf of the President of the United States of America in honour of your son." Funerals in America were treated with great respect. The car in which I travelled formed part of a motorcade and two police outriders stopped all other traffic and allowed us to pass through the red lights. People stopped and paid their respects as we made our way to the cemetery.

During our stay I was invited to address the Rotary. The proprietor of an ice cream parlour invited us to his parlour to have anything which whetted our appetite, "on the house". We have never seen such a splendid array of different ice cream, over forty varieties. Waitresses wore the most cheeky straw boaters and white blouses, with coloured garters on their white stockings. We had a banana split ice cream, laced with cream and strawberry juice, each bearing the American flag.

A visit to Oregon, where many of the great western cowboy films were made, would be incomplete without going to a rodeo, featuring displays by skilled cowboys of bareback riding, steer roping, wild cow milking and, most dangerous of all, riding wild bulls. It was a thrill a second. We were on the edge of our seats as the cowboy was released from an enclosure into the ring on a horse that was kicking its front and back legs high in the air almost at the same time. The dust rose and suddenly the cowboy was biting the dust as he fell to the ground with a look of puzzled surprise on his face, his Stetson having fallen off in the struggle One after the other went into the ring and on this occasion I never saw a cowboy's victory!

One early morning we went to what was called a "buckaroo" breakfast. It consisted of a delicious pancake with lashings of syrup, fried eggs, and coffee – all of this for $1 – and we ate to the pleasant sound of cowboy singers.

An excellent movement at the Eugene church was "Brave Christians". I had never heard of this movement before but it brought new life to the church and apparently was in many parts of the American Methodist church. It was open to all who desired to live a disciplined Christian life. The group met on Thursday evenings for prayer and Bible study over coffee and cookies, exchanging the week's experiences. There were five disciplines, the two hardest being the tithing of ten per cent of one's income and rising at 5.30 a.m. each morning for prayer and meditation on the word of God.

Alan Maxwell, a leader of the group, a successful and wealthy businessman, was the main inspiration. Many of the young people in the church, in the 14–18 age group, had given their lives to Christ. When I heard some of the stories of their encounter with Jesus I was deeply moved. As Samuel Johnson once said: "Wonders are willingly told and willingly heard"; to listen to these testimonies was refreshing and inspiring, and if we went to America just to get firsthand knowledge of the "Brave Christian Movement" our journey would not have been in vain.

We arranged a barbecue for all the young people at the home of a leading florist. We had games and lots of fun and afterwards we sat on the verandah of the house and sang choruses. I was so impressed with this movement that I determined when I returned home I would start it in my own church.

While we were in Eugene we went to California and saw the redwood trees, some being among the highest trees in the world and some 6,000 years old. Walt Disney made the film *Tom Thumb* among the redwood trees. A much smaller tree was the myrtlewood tree, the rarest wood in the world. They grow only on the southern Oregon coast and in the Holy Land. The wood was extremely hard and finely textured, full of colourful swirls and designs. Each piece of wood was different and required an experienced craftsman to select the best art form to bring out the hidden beauty. Oregon was noted for its trees. These were felled and taken by road or train or down the river to the large lumber mills for processing into planks, plywood, and paper. It was a unique experience to go through the mill and watch tree trunks weighing several tons being flipped about like matchsticks and sawn by great saws into various size planks.

On the way back to Eugene we saw a signpost pointing towards Goshen, so named after the Goshen mentioned in the Old Testament, the section of North East Egypt where the hungry Jacob family of seventy persons settled at the behest of the Pharaoh's Prime Minister, Joseph. The early settlers were deeply religious people.

We visited Crater Lake, one of the world's most beautiful lakes, covering more than 21 square miles. It was discovered in 1853 by John Wesley Hillman. The lake was 1,932 feet deep and of the deepest blue, but icy cold all the year round and far too dangerous for swimming.

We were warned to stay away from the wild bears, and, since we were there for the night, we never ventured out in the dark.

A lady Methodist minister took us to the Pacific coast, where we spent a delightful day in a small cabin overlooking the ocean. In the afternoon we searched for driftwood and found some most exciting shapes that we decided to take home with us.

Our final service at Eugene Methodist Church was a memorable one. I was presented with a wooden plaque with the words engraved in brass: "God's messenger who brought us spiritual strength and the truth that Jesus is alive today". Betty and Jane were given gifts as an expression of love, and in addition we had a special collection from the people of the church. Our final hymn was: "God be with you till we meet again". After the service we gathered in the fellowship hall where an enormous iced cake with the words "Farewell to the Bowers", had been prepared. It was an emotional parting.

We left Eugene and stayed the night in New York and then caught the VC10 to Manchester, where we were met by our friend Watson. We will never forget our visit to America and the beautiful city of Eugene where the magnificent cross on a hilltop overlooked the city, the arms of which stretched out pointing from east to west, a reminder that the whole world was linked together by Christ, who makes all good things possible, and who alone was the Saviour of the world. Many young people in the church gave their lives to Christ as a result of the Brave Christian Movement and the church, which had once lost members, became vibrant and strong again.

We were reminded of our six wonderful weeks exchange visit to America at a special gathering in our Lower Bebington Church when I gave an illustrated talk with slides. I played a recording of the voice of Gerald Williams, our host during our stay:

Greetings from the "Wild West". We were pleased to have the ministry of the Rev and Mrs Allan J. Bowers, and we have many fond memories of their short stay with us. One of the things I think Allan found difficult to get used to was the extreme heat. It wasn't long before he began to adopt the ways of the natives, and took off his clerical collar, and wore a loose sports shirt and Betty even borrowed my wife's shorts. Allan came the day after his arrival and asked us if there was something about the heating system he did not understand because it seemed unusually warm to him. Well, upon making a few enquiries it was discovered that not only was the temperature very high outside but the central heating in the house was going at full blast. Missionaries going to central Africa are fully aware of the risks of being boiled alive but in coming to the USA one may expect to run into Red Indians occasionally but one doesn't expect to be met by cannibals!

The evening of talk and slides was enjoyed, and it was then that I said I hoped to start the Brave Christian Movement in our church. Shortly after my return I started the movement and wrote an article about it for the *Methodist Recorder*. In response to this article I received many letters. A lady from Leeds wrote: "I know that a regular prayer time is essential and so I decided to do it before my marriage and the twenty minutes I began with became an hour and a half before breakfast each day. After marriage and a young family it was impossible for me to continue, but now that my children were grown up I wish to get back to a disciplined prayer life." A minister from Cockermouth wrote: "One of my resolutions was to make an attempt to strengthen the spiritual life"

Chapter Fifteen

This Is Your Life

Our stay in Bebington came to a close with a specially arranged "This is your Life" evening, before a large audience. Some of our family were secretly hidden away and to our surprise Donald Singleton and Ron Owens, lay workers in a most interesting way, brought messages from our previous churches. My brother, Stanley, who could not be with us on this occasion sent the following message:

I'm here in spirit in order to say something of the distant past when we were young brothers together in London in the twenties and thirties, that is before I left home to become a candidate for the Methodist ministry through the adventurous channels which in those days were called "Lay Pastor". Curiously enough, those years of childhood together seem so remote that they might have taken place in another world altogether. The one thing that stood out most vividly was our Granddad Mogg, called you "rubber face", and most frequently declared that one day you would be a parson. How prophetic he turned out to be! You always loved talking a lot, and if my memory was to be relied upon, you could talk yourself out of every situation that arose in our family of four small children, all very young together. No doubt you were even then in early training for all the skills required in taking the chair of troublesome Trustees' meetings or Circuit Quarterly Meetings in which the new assessments were debated. As you know I have been an Anglican priest for ten years now but I've not forgotten Methodism. I remember how you used to play at chapels, weddings and funerals, and used tiny egg cups for communion services. Yes, the thought of ministering to people was in your blood from the start, and I am glad that I had some part in your coming into the Methodist Ministry. Later when you had to join the Royal Air Force, I was a probationer minister in North Devon. I clearly recall the deep and prolonged talks we had into the early morning when our cities were being smashed by enemy aircraft. We really thought we had solved all the inexhaustible problems of Theology.

The Reverend Dr Gordon Barritt, MA, OBE, Principal of the National Children's Home, sent this message:

Greetings to you, Allan, on this special occasion. You will recall that we met many years ago when we were in the Royal Air Force, and now I find myself Principal of the National Children's Home. Of course, the 1940s are a long time ago and it isn't easy to remember all the details of those days, perhaps that's as well! We were both on a training course and I discovered that you had come from some very trying experiences and I was impressed by the strength of your Christian convictions and the strong sense of call you had to the ministry; this was a great help for I too was a candidate and think you were the only other candidate I met at that time, so we had a lot in common. As I look back I remember you as an extremely good looking young man, very slim and studious because you always seemed to have a Theological book under your arm. I was never quite sure how you managed to get away with the sergeant, but somehow or other you did. Over the years we have met on one or two occasions. Once in Sheffield when I visited your church to preach, before lunch we started talking about old times, and then after lunch you became ill, and I was never quite sure whether I was to blame for this! Well, Allan, I'm delighted to send greetings to you on this special occasion. If we don't quite look as we did thirty years ago, well, at least, we never had doubts about being ministers. I am sure that you are having a wonderful time, and I wish that I could be with you. Every blessing for the future and don't forget to take a "League of Light Box" with you wherever you go.

A lady who became a dear friend, Muriel Willmott, had a lasting influence upon me. As previously mentioned, I met her when I went to live at the Home Farm, Willersley Castle. She recorded this message for the "This Is Your Life" evening:

As I sit at the table all alone, speaking into the microphone, I look at the picture that you painted for me in 1948. It has always accompanied me to our various Guild Guest Houses as I have journeyed around, and now it's in my cottage of retirement. How the years have flown since those happy days at Willersley Castle, and now as I talk to you both I can see you, Allan, popping in occasionally for a chat. In the early days I used to think you were coming to see me, but soon realized that Betty was the real attraction. I remember at that time I was the Society Steward at our Via Gellia chapel in the Matlock Trinity Circuit, and we were concerned at finding digs for this new young minister who was coming to us. I feel sure you must have been divinely led when we hit upon the idea of having rooms made available for you in the Home Farm at the bottom of the drive, and it was in this way we got to know you so well and grew so fond of you. Whether Betty ever walked you home at night I shall never know, but if she did I'm sure you walked her back again. I don't ever remember her being locked out. I was so happy to see your friendship grow into love, and I know over the years your love has deepened for both of you and you have been used by God in that wonderful ministry. Betty was very kind and let me have you to myself on some occasions, and some of my happiest memories were those conversations we had on spiritual matters, sometimes going on for too long and beyond locking up time. But you were a tower of strength for all of us who worked at Willersley, and I know for sure that God used you in my life, to bring me into a closer relationship with him. Two words which have stayed with me, and came out of our talking of the deeper things of life were "Victorious Living". How I tried to live up to it, but how I failed, but those two words lingered helpfully and inspiringly with me, and I still try to tread the victorious path of life. And now Betty and Allan, as you say "Goodbye" to all your friends where you have been so happy, I must say how pleased I am to share with you tonight in these celebrations, and as you leave for a new church in the Wolverhampton area I pray God's blessing upon you. Thank you for all the fun we have had together, for the fellowship, and thank you above all for our friendship.

That friendship continued through the years until her death, when I was privileged to conduct her memorial service at Sidholme Methodist Guild House, where she served devotedly for a number of years. Whenever she wrote to us she put at the end of her letter, "Victorious Living".

Ron and Donald had been in touch with my former college tutor at Hartley Victoria Theological College, the Reverend Dr Percy Scott. He had this to say: "Allan Bowers was a boyish looking student when he came to college in 1948. He was unusual because of his artistic ability, especially painting, which I presume he has kept up. He studied conscientiously, and frequently asked interesting and intelligent questions and also made his own discerning comments." He also recalled that the course of true love never did run smooth, and he went on to say: "I recollect when a young lady in whom he was deeply interested had doubts, he was a sorry sight for several days, but if I remember rightly, he was a persistent swain and I believe they eventually married and lived happily ever after."

While I was at college I made many friends, one of whom was John Creber, who eventually became Principal Chaplain in the Royal Navy and was made an OBE for his distinguished services. He said:

In case any friends listening associate Hartley Victoria College croquet with a picture of Victorian ladies gliding gracefully round a green lawn at teatime, and perhaps smiling at the thought of Allan or anyone else playing croquet, it was a lethal game. It was certainly a safety valve for men, many of whom had seen service in the Second World War, and it enabled them to let off steam under the pressure of a greatly condensed college course. Consequently, although it may have happened in Theological seminars, there was no mercy shown or expected on the croquet lawns of Hartley. Tempers occasionally wore thin but Allan was one of those who never appeared to get ruffled or take a wicked delight in smashing an opponent's croquet ball as far out of the game as possible. This is why I tell this story, because one's attitude to games is often true of one's attitude to life. Allan, as a student, was always cheerful, friendly, and helpful. To sum it up, he remained a perfect gentleman through all the stresses and strains of the particularly difficult years. It is great to speak to you now; we haven't met for many years, but I expect you kept a gentle eye on those you knew at Hartley, as I have done myself, and you will know that I am now in the Royal navy and have remained a service Chaplain for twenty-four years, whereas you came in for a few years and then went back to the civilian ministry again, at the heart of the same brotherhood of Methodist ministers. May God bless you, Betty and Allan, may the undoubted happiness of this particular evening that you are sharing be reflected in many years of future ministry together. I hope that one of these days we shall have the opportunity of meeting again.

Messages of good wishes were read from those who had known me at Sheffield. Jack Pike was a steward there, and he had this to say:

The thing that stood out in my memory of our first meeting and informal chat was Allan's intense desire to know all about Hillsborough Trinity Church, and this took place the day after his arrival at the manse when everything was upside down. His enthusiasm for work soon became apparent and continued throughout the six years he was with us. It was his desire to make the church a caring society, and to this end he encouraged us to embark on a lay pastoral visitation scheme which brought many of the fringe friends to become more actively engaged in the fellowship. Within two years of his coming we opened the new church hall, which stands as a monument to his faith and impatient enthusiasm. These are but two examples of many facets of his work with us. Time does not allow to extend these remarks; he abounded in Christian love and his friendly smile and warm handshake showed his sincerity of purpose. The support given to him by his wife Betty was of inestimable value to him in the large amound of work she did behind the scenes.

Ted Rowley, another of the stewards at Hillsborough Trinity, had this to say:

I first met Allan and his charming wife, Betty, soon after they arrived at the manse in Sheffield. I was soon to appreciate his sincerity and the strength of his spiritual conviction. He was a strong believer in Methodist–Anglican Unity and the Ecumenical movement generally. It was his inspiration that led to a "Watchman Scheme" of pastoral visitation and care and the formation of "House Groups".

Sidney Booth, who later became chairman of the Sheffield District, had this to say:

You may not remember, Betty, but long ago, probably more years than you care to remember, actually it was in July 1949, I met you at Willersley Castle. You were secretary. It was, therefore, a delight when in 1961 Allan and you joined the circuit where I was already a minister. I seem to remember, Allan, at one time in the cellars of Hillsborough Trinity, we were searching among all sorts of rubble looking for some documents that we never found, although we did find a lot of things that we didn't really want. Staff meetings in those days were quite interesting with poor old Norman Boulton, who was not well at the time, dropping off to sleep in his chair and letting the rest of us get on with it. I recall that you had an odd idea about outer space. Do you still have funny ideas? Probably you do. Your ideas, however, as the Chapel Secretary, were far from funny, and when you became Chapel Secretary of the Sheffield District you set a pattern and method of orderliness which continued long after you left.

Joan Plant, a delightful soul, reminded us of a picture postcard that I sent to her while on holiday in Devon. It has these words of wisdom on it: "My advice to you, me dears, is don't ye worry, just take your time, there's no need at all to hurry and shouldn't some things go exactly quiet, all the worry in the world won't put them right, so do the best with all your might and don't ye worry". She went on to remind the gathering of an incident that took place in Sheffield.

Do you remember, Allan, when you were stuck in the snow on New Year's Day at Bradfield? I'm sure the snow shifters would never have used such bad language if they had seen your dog collar, which was concealed by your overcoat. Yes, you caught a cold, but thanks to Langdale Cinnamon Essence we managed to revive you before Betty returned from her mother's.

That memorable night of "This Is Your Life" there was one more voice to be heard, that of Mrs Ann Fellows, wife of Cedric, one of our ministers.

I'm sure you recognize the voice. Do you remember in 1964, when Betty and you installed me as Queen Forget-Me-Not, what a happy day that was? It was you who sowed so many seeds in the lives of young people of the Bible Class, resulting in many of them giving their hearts to Jesus, and that wonderful Easter Sunday morning, I think it was 1966, when you received some into membership, including Cedric, you also persuaded us to start a mission band, which is still operating today through a new generation of people, even after nine years. And you quietly watched our courtship grow. I think you rather enjoyed that, in fact you were the first person we ever told of our intended engagement. Do you remember the 6th of September was our wedding day, and I was twenty minutes late for the service because the door fell off the taxi on the way to church? And I'd promised you I would be there on time! You gave us a wonderful start to our marriage, that's why we have been so happy ever since. They are all happy memories, but I think most of all I remember your happy smiling face, your boundless enthusiasm and your genuine concern for people, and the encouragement you gave to us all, especially the young ones. Most of all, I remember you for the way you saw God in the ordinary things of life. Cedric and I even today talk about the sermon on the blocked drain. Do you remember it? It ws after we had sung to you on Christmas Eve and had blocked up your drains with tea leaves and eaten all your mince pies. Or the box for further light, and being King's walkers and not just King's talkers, just to mention a few. You once described a saint as being someone through whom God's light shines. I'm sure he shines through you and I know he always will.

The "This Is Your Life" evening closed after the giving of gifts to each of us, a token of the friendship and affection of the friends. Our ministry in Bebington was one of the happiest experiences, perhaps because it was my first superintendency. As I stepped into this new office, with greater responsibility, I wondered if I could handle it, but once again I realized that the power of God was available for all who "trust and obey", and, what was always so wonderful and enriching, the strength and love that radiates from fellow Christians keeps one's spirits up and keeps one going. And so we left Bebington after seven happy years.

Chapter Sixteen

Codsall

In August 1974 we arrived at Codsall, our next appointment, on the outskirts of Wolverhampton, on the border of the Shropshire countryside. I was appointed as the superintendent minister of the Wolverhampton Trinity circuit, where again I followed my friend, the Reverend George Moralee. The Codsall church was in an area of development where young executives employed in Wolverhampton were having their homes built. It was a pleasant area and so near to beautiful country. The church was strong, with a Sunday School of 250 children and thirty teachers. The manse was set back in a beautiful garden, a stone's throw from the church. Unfortunately, I arrived at a time when the church had to ask their minister to leave, because of an affair he had with a married woman in the congregation, and this meant a Discipline Committee and his resignation from the ministry. I soon discovered that the church was split in its fellowship; there were some for the minister, and others against him. Methodism views these matters with great seriousness, and there was no avoiding the minister having to appear before the Discipline Committee. However, the rules made it clear that there would be an opportunity for him to apply for reinstatement after a year or two, if the circumstances permitted and searching questions had been answered satisfactorily.

I found prayers to be said on behalf of the injured parties and the minister: "Guide, O Lord, the straying shepherd back to the fold, and assist him to walk surely and lovingly in your sight, for only in union with you will he find true light, joy and peace. Give to all ministers inspiration in time of doubt, patience in time of adversity, fortitude in time of weakness, that with your love ever pressing them on, they may lead others closer to you."

I am pleased to say that with much prayer and understanding the church fellowship became united again and the minister in question was forgiven by his wife and found employment that was satisfying and fulfilling, but he never returned to the ministry.

During my first year at Codsall I was introduced to the mayor of Wolverhampton, who wore his splendid gold chain of office. I noticed that the motto on the the chain was, "From darkness to light". The inspiration for the motto must have come from the Bible, 1 Peter: 2: 9: "But you are a chosen race, a royal priesthood, a holy nation, God's own people, that you may declare the wonderful deeds of him who called you out of darkness into his marvellous light". Such, in a way, was my task after the church's very difficult time, by the grace of God to bring it out of darkness into light.

Our first year in Codsall witnessed a baby boom. I cannot remember baptizing so many babies before. The church became strong, with a membership of almost three hundred. The Women's Fellowship reached over a hundred members. The secretary, Mrs Keen, was Keen by name and keen by nature. If anyone was missing on Monday afternoon she would be on the telephone that evening and a visit would take place. Everyone was cared for and loved.

Wherever I have been stationed, I have started a prayer meeting. Codsall was no exception, and we met on Tuesday evening for what we called a "Power, Praise and Prayer meeting". It was well attended, and became the powerhouse of the church. We believed that God was best known and his will decided at the prayer meeting.

It was at Codsall that I first started healing services. The first was held at evening worship. I recall at my ordination these words spoken by the President: "I hereby declare you to be ordained to the Holy Ministry, hold up the weak, heal the sick, bind up the broken, bring again the outcasts, seek the lost." Throughout my ministry I have thought of the church as the healing church, its ministry of healing going out into the world in so many ways, healing not only bodies but societies, releasing people from pain and sin, enabling them by the power of Christ to walk in newness of life.

The service included the sacrament of Holy Communion and the Word of God was preached before people were invited to come forward for the laying on of hands. These services were held at intervals of three months until we launched into deeper waters of the healing ministry and invited the Reverend Trevor Dearing to conduct a special healing service following several meetings for prayer at our Tuesday evening "Power, Prayer and Healing Meeting". Between four and five hundred people from Codsall, Wolverhampton, Birmingham and Crewe came together to praise God and wait upon him in prayer. Instead of the traditional hour of Methodist worship on a Sunday, the special service went on for over three hours, with singing, corporate prayer, speaking in tongues, and the healing ministry. It was a moving experience to see dozens of people come forward for healing, some who found difficulty in walking, and some in wheelchairs, children in the arms of parents, the blind, deaf, and mentally sick. After the laying on of hands several at a time were lying on the floor within the communion rail, under the healing power of God. The Reverend Trevor Deaing and his team and many present were seeking to co-operate with God in the healing ministry, just as the surgeons, doctors, psychiatrists, nurses, and social workers seek healing for the people under their care. Those present witnessed many dedicating and rededicating their lives to God. The meeting closed with an act of prayer and praise as the entire congregation filled the communion area, gathered beneath the cross. Hands were clasped in friendship and love as everyone joined in singing "Spirit of the living God, fall afresh on me". The service of Power, Prayer and Healing closed as the Lord's Prayer was said by all and Trevor Dearing gave the blessing, but as some remained behind for further counselling the remainder of the congregation left. I knew that the ministry would continue with trust in Christ, who was able to do far more than we could ask or think.

These services were not without criticism and in some respects made some people feel that they should no longer be held. However, we persisted, believing that God willed the healing ministry for his Church and certain that new ideas centered on the question of healing would turn out to be illuminating if pursued in the spirit of prayer. There were many experts on the unknowable, but who could say what revelations would come in understanding what "healing" really was as more people in various aspects of healing waited upon God for guidance. There was evidence that the Roman Catholic Church expected miracles of healing to happen, especially at the shrine of Lourdes, which spoke of definite cures. The whole question of spiritual healing had been discussed by all the mainstream churches and in recent years had come to be practised by all the churches in one form or another. It is recognized by the medical profession that man is a "psychosomatic unity" and that in dealing with medical matters it is necessary to take into consideration the whole person, and, since all healing is ultimately a gift of God, co-operate with those engaged in spiritual matters. It would be wonderful indeed if this took place in every town and city in the land. I am sure that many doctors, nurses, and social workers would be happy to see this happen, but there is, in my view, a persistent temptation, when considering medical resources as a whole, to suppose that there is a mechanical solution to all disease and to forget the value and worth of people as human beings. Dietrich Bonhoeffer, a modern saint, wrote: "Only a suffering God can help". What we started at our Codsall church was an attempt to let people know that the "crucified Jesus was the one accurate picture of God the world had ever seen", and that fixing our eyes on Jesus and remembering his ministry of compassion and healing, he sets before us an example.

Sadly, during the second year of our stay in Codsall, Betty's mother became ill and we had to take her to a nursing home in Wolverhampton for special care. We were reluctant to do this, but she needed round-the-clock nursing, and died soon after on 13th August, 1975. The funeral service was held in the Weston-on-Trent village Methodist chapel where she and the family worshipped for many years. I was privileged to share in the service with Reverend

George Farnell of Matlock. A song, a favourite of Betty's mother, was sung by a friend, the words I often heard her mother sing in the family home: "I would have the Saviour with me, / For I dare not walk alone, / I would feel his presence near me, / And his arm around me thrown".

In November 1976, Betty and I celebrated our Silver Wedding and the church arranged a special evening for the celebration and provided us with gifts and a sumptuous meal.

Later that year six other couples celebrated their silver wedding and we had a special thanksgiving service which was taken by my colleague, the Reverend Nigel Collinson.

The same year I was privileged to share in the marriage service of Graham Kendrick, who later became famous for his hymns and songs sung at large annual gatherings for events like Spring Harvest.

During my stay in the Wolverhampton Trinity circuit I arranged a yearly circuit week-end at Willersley Castle. The first one, in March 1977, was on the theme: "The Family of Christ". It was was shared by Nigel and was an immediate success.

It was at this time that I began writing hymns for church services and was given practical help and encouragement by the Reverend Dr Green, who readily looked at some of my early hymns and offered wise advice and helpful comments for which I shall always be grateful.

Our daughter, Jane, joined the Hillsborough Trinity Drama Group, which was called: "The Histon Players". To our delight she appeared in a number of plays. She excelled herself as a young actress with considerable flair, unlike her father, who at the men's weekend plays called: "Mental Mania", could never remember his lines, which always made the audiences roar with laughter.

On the 2nd February, 1978 my brother Stanley rang from Bristol to tell me that our beloved father had died very peacefully in his favourite armchair. He was a truly wonderful father and I owed him my loyalty and devotion. He was in every way a lovely man and his passing, like that of my mother, filled me with pain, but that is the price we all pay for the passing of a loved one. Betty and I went to the funeral on a crisp, cold day on the 10th of February and we were joined by his devoted second wife, Ivy, and Stanley and Ruth, Grace and Edward, and our two half-brothers, Peter and Christopher.

Hilda was unable to join us from Germany. The minister in his address spoke about "Going home". As much as our father loved Ivy, who looked after him so well, he did say that no one could take the place of our mother, who was his first love. Our three cousins, Percy, Len and Rene also came to the funeral.

While at Codsall I joined the Institute of Religion and Medicine and attended the yearly conferences. One which I found most interesting was held at The Queens College, Birmingham. The subject was "Expertise and Experience". There I met Dr Malcolm Rigler, with whom I had been in correspondence. With considerable courage he had started a new style of medical practice that involved patient participation. His method was a change in the perception of expertise and experience. He believed patient participation would be a step forward in healing.

During my final year in Codsall there was increased talk of nuclear war. I could not get out of my mind the effects of a single atomic bomb on Hiroshima in 1945, which I referred to earlier when I recorded my visit to that ancient Japanese city. Nuclear war, should it ever be waged affecting our country, would cause indescribable damage and unimaginable death and destruction from which it would take many generations to recover, if it ever did.

Only twice have I had a letter published in *The Times*, one on the allowances of a Methodist minister, suggesting that, as in Germany, they be paid through a small tax, and the other on the peril of nuclear warfare. On the question of nuclear warfare I made the following points:

1. The urgent need for our time was for a workable international law administered by a world authority that would not be defeated by individual nations who claimed to be judges in their own cause. At the present time the United Nations, splendid organization that it was, appeared to be powerless in the face of such events as we have seen in Iran and Afghanistan.

2. A fact of supreme importance is that in our time there is in existence a worldwide spiritual community, which transcends race,
colour, nationality and all the divisive political ideologies. It is
surely the most potent force making for peace and justice and
the brotherhood of mankind. Could not the new Archbishop of
Canterbury, Dr Runcie, call a religious summit meeting of the
top spiritual leaders in the world to seek God's guidance in this
dangerous situation and give the ordinary minister and lay
person a lead?

I followed up this letter in a day or so by sending the following
telegram to Dr Robert Runcie, Archbishop of Canterbury: "My con-
gratulations upon your enthronement. You can be assured of my
prayers. See my letter in *The Times* (22nd March 1980)".
Dr Runcie replied as follows;

Dear Mr Bowers,

I thought you should know that your letter to *The Times* of March
22nd has not gone unnoticed.

I share your feelings of despair at the escalation of armaments and the
peril of nuclear warfare; but you will know that this does call for
some hard thinking as well as a staunch determination to do something about it. I hope that you will have been encouraged by a speech
made by Cardinal Hume on Saturday.

As for myself, I am drawing together a group of people to advise me
about the sort of contribution that I am able to make.

This is not the same as calling for a Religious Summit, but is serious
preparatory work so that I may have something to say and some
encouragement to give in what I agree to be the most serious ethical
problem of the day.

So I hope you will be patient. I am not asleep about this issue.

Yours sincerely,
Robert Canterbury

Among the many letters I received was one from T. M. Heron, dated 25th March 1980, enclosing a copy of a letter he had written to the Archbishop, as follows:

My dear Archbishop,

The letter from Rev. Allan Bowers in Saturday's *Times* (March 22nd) emboldens me to write and say how very much I hope you may see your way to accede to his request, and call a Religious Summit Meeting to seek God's guidance concerning the very serious situation which has arisen as a result of the Russian invasion of Afghanistan.

At the end of the copy of the letter he wrote:

Harold MacMillan would back your request. He had an agonizing time persuading the American President and the Russians to install the "hot line telephone" between Washington and Moscow and each to promise that they would not be first to drop the bomb and if it was set off by mistake to pay the damage and not retaliate. Both Governments are anxious not to have a war. But what worries me now is that the governments seem to have no common purpose.

It was in those last days at Codsall that I realized more than ever that the existence of nuclear weapons was an abomination, an outrage to God, to nature, and to humanity. I believe, however, that the correspondence in *The Times* did get the ball rolling to make people think that our spiritual nature could prevail over the material forces of destruction, given the will under the mighty grace and power of God.

In the summer of 1978 we decided it would be a valuable investment to buy a property in Sidmouth to be used for holidays and possibly for our eventual retirement. We both liked Sidmouth and since my short spell in the RAF in Sidmouth in 1942, when I stayed at the Royal Glen Hotel, my desire to retire there one day had grown. And so we spent a week at the Sidmount Hotel looking for properties and eventually decided to buy a Georgian house, in Drake's Avenue for the sum of £22,000. Our original intention was to buy a bungalow, but bungalows at that time were in great demand and none was available. It was while spending a summer holiday that same year at the new house, which we called "Byes Lodge" that Ralph Ravenhall, the Circuit Steward of Sidmouth and Bridport Circuit telephoned me and asked if I would be interested in coming to Sidmouth and Bridport as the Superintendent minister in September 1980, when I was due to leave the Woverhampton Trinity Circuit. My reply was that I would give the invitation prayerful consideration, but I didn't think I would be able to say yes because I had been used to ministering to one large church and didn't relish the idea of a rural circuit and to have pastoral care of five churches as well as the superintendency.

Meanwhile, while attending the Division of Property Meeting in Manchester, I discovered that that there was a set of plans for the building of a new church in the seaside town of Seaton, in Devon, just ten miles from Sidmouth. When next at Byes Lodge Betty and I decided to go and look at the manse at Axminster and meet the Superintendent Minister, Keith Parsons, an ex-China missionary. Though we didn't like the manse we warmed to the prospect of a new church at Seaton. There was only £5,000 available, a site would have to be purchased in Seaton, and an enormous sum of money raised for the new building. We gave the matter a great deal of prayer and finally decided to accept the invitation to move to Axminster, be involved in the building of a new church, and take on the superintendency. Betty was fully behind the move, although I knew she didn't relish moving from a lovely manse and a strong church at Codsall. The idea of being involved in the building of a new church pursued me, and so I was reconciled to moving to Axminster.

Our many friends at Codsall and in the Wolverhampton Trinity Circuit gave us a splendid farewell at our Codsall church, attended by the Chairman of the district, Reverend Nigel Gilson, DFC, MA, and my colleague Reverend Nigel Collinson, MA.

John Donson, the senior steward at our Codsall church, had some nice things to say about both of us. He reminded us that we had come to the church at a difficult time, but through faith, drive, and enthusiasm the church had been lifted to a new awareness and the numbers of worshippers had steadily increased. He said there were too many things to list for which they would always be grateful, and especially the Day Care Centre that Betty had started and her encouragement in the work of the Women's Fellowship and the Tuesday Evening Club. John referred to my light-hearted performances in Mental Mania, as Friar Chipps, Cannon Bull, and Cardinal Polish, and the odd odes I gave from time to time.

The Chairman, after our farewell, wrote of our "courtesy" at all times, and the warmth of our hospitality. On behalf of the District he expressed sincere appreciation for work done at District and Connexional levels.

By now "remembrance of things past" had turned into "reflection on things present and things to come". Looking back thus far things have come vividly to mind, helped by my diary that I kept each day. Now we were about to move to new fields of endeavour and I wondered how things would work out.

Chapter Seventeen

Axminster and Seaton

On the day we moved from Codsall it was hot, so hot that a candle in the conservatory of the new manse melted. Jane helped with the unpacking of the many boxes, and remarked on several occasions that she thought we had lost our senses in this new move, the manse and the area being so vastly different from that at Codsall. The Axminster manse was over a hundred years old; there were rats scratching at night under the floorboards and snail trails appeared in the study in the mornings. However, we felt that God had called us into this situaton and he would guide us as we started an entirely new ministry. I had hoped to continue studies for a London University Bachelor of Divinity degree, but I decided this would have to be delayed for the time being.

I had supervised the building of a regimental church on the banks of the River Imjin after the war in Korea was over; now I was to supervise the building of a new church in Seaton. The little church at Colyford was bursting at the seams, although some years earlier the membership had been reduced to five and the church came near to closing. I really do believe that "God moves in a mysterious way his wonders to perform", and although we had no idea where the money was coming from to start this new enterprise, we believed that where God guides he also provides. The church at Colyford was situated behind the Wheelwright Café, the small site having been purchased for the sum of £5 from a local butcher. The chapel had cob walls, thatched roof, and a stone floor. Twice the chapel closed, in 1850 and again in 1866, and never had more than fifteen members until the 1960s, when concentrated pastoral care from two retired ministers, Edgar Perry and John Stanfield, brought the members up to seventy.

The story goes that one day John Stanfield was resting on a five-barred gate, looking across the field, and in a moment of vision and faith he said to himself, "One day this will be the site of a new Methodist Church." And so it came to pass. Betty and I stayed in Axminster for one year, and through the good offices of the Property Developer, Mr Douglas Cotrill, a site for a new manse was obtained in Poplar Tree Drive and work started on this at the same time as work started on the new site for the church.

A great deal of prayer, preparation and faith preceded the actual obtaining of the site and the building of the church. The church will always be grateful to Mr Henry Davis, at that time in his eighties, who persuaded the East Devon District Council to sell the site, valued at £40,000, for the sum of £10,000 because it was for a church. The site was conveyed at the end of September 1980, and the fresh green turf of the field was cut within a few days. So the building of the church began, but it was to be a church built through the good offices of a projection team, a local builder as a clerk of works, and under the direction of Mr Francis Bush, an architect from Plymouth. Local labour on a sub-contracted basis was used. In addition to paid labour, a volunteer force of church members worked very hard to produce substantial savings by interior decorating. I don't recall, during my many years on the Division of Property, seeing any other plans throughout Methodism for the building of a church such as the one at Seaton. It was my firm belief that God brought together men and women from different walks of life and from other parts of the country to live in Seaton so as to make the new church possible, people with business skills and wide experience.

A key man in this project was Mr Ken Cox, who had been District Planning Officer for Bristol and who had come to live in Seaton. Mr

Henry Davis, a Local Preacher for many years, with considerable experience as a councillor, Mr Ken Shepherd, a salesman for a large brick manufacturing firm, who supplied the bricks and acted as Liaison Officer, Mr Francis Bush, architect, gifted in designing modern churches and a keen Methodist, Mr Victor Ansell, an astute treasurer, Mr Stanley Cogswell, joint treasurer and organist, and myself as the minister, were styled by the local press as "The Magnificent Seven".

The architect gave us a caravan and this was placed on the site and a telephone was installed. The Clerk of Works was Mr Basil Lang, who, under the direction of the architect, employed local labour for the building of the church. The design of the church attracted wide attention and commendation. It was to be distinctive without being elaborate. I recall early in the laying of the foundations the Clerk of Works saying one day that there was a "hotline to heaven". It was his way of saying that prayer combined with action

"The Magnificent Seven"

achieved more than words could say. I'm sure he would have warmed to the words of Nehemiah, who rebuilt the walls of Jerusalem. And I am sure, as was my experience in building a church for our soliders in Korea, that many people found themselves helped when they were allowed to play the helper. At first we envisaged that £125,000 would complete the scheme, but as the days and weeks passed we knew that the final sum was going to be many thousands of pounds more. As I have commented before, a former Chancellor of the Exchequer had said, "Money is the root of all progress", and that is true. We know that money opens many doors, but faith opens even more doors.

It was quite amazing how the money kept coming, small amounts from pensioners and large amounts from outside sources. The name of Rank will be known by many people as the great film entrepreneur, but he was also a great benefactor of Methodism. I was fortunate in meeting his son-in-law, Mr Paul Bartlett Lang, on the Board of Trustees for Methodist Church Purposes, and to have lunch with him in Manchester. Over lunch, when I acquainted him with our desperate need for money, he said he would recommend to the Division of Property that through the Joseph Rank Benevolent Trust we should receive £25,000 towards the new church. I never enjoyed a lunch quite so much as that one. At the same time as we were spending large sums of money our overdraft at the Midland Bank in Seaton was growing until at its peak we were overdrawn to the sum of one hundred thousand pounds. The Regional Director was on our side, but there was a limit to what we could borrow and at the same time inflation was so high that bank charges rose to around 22%. At night Betty would turn to me, unable to sleep, and wonder how we would be able to find the money and pay the interest charges.

Fortunately for us, but not so for the Branscombe Methodists, their church, after a life of eighty-five years, had to close. Some said the circuit had put pressure on the Branscombe church to close but as I said to the press at the time, the future of the Branscombe church was already under consideration by the circuit. For the last ten years there had been no growth situation. There was a congregation of around five and the numbers were so small that services were held in a tiny hall while the main church remained empty and unused throughout the winter, with all the deterioration to the fabric that was taking place as a result. And so, reluctantly, the church was sold and the sum of £30,000 obtained in the sale, a large proportion of which went towards the new church.

At the same time as we required money for the church building we also needed to find £42,000 for the building of the new manse. The saying: "It never rains but it pours" seemed true, because the property developer wanted the deposit for the new manse at the same time as the bank wanted more security against the overdraft for the church. Permission was given to sell the manse at Axminster where we had lived for a year, but the circuit insisted that the money should be in hand before a contract was signed for the new manse. I recall one sunny morning standing outside the manse at Axminster where a "For Sale" notice had been placed, wondering whether we would ever get a sale. It was an old house and not terribly attractive to look at. A lady approached me and asked me if I was fit for viewing, whereupon I smiled and told her I was, I hoped, always fit for viewing. The house was sold for the sum of £30,000 but we still needed £12,000 to complete the purchase for the new manse.

Providence is never far away, I firmly believe. I attended a meeting of the Connexional Advance Committee in London, of which I was a member, chaired by Donald English, who, when I brought my begging bowl for the Seaton manse, asked me to present the case. I arrived home that night with a cheque for £8,000. All I required was £4,000 and I would be home and dry. I sat that night in my study and with some trepidation rang four friends in the circuit to request a loan of £1,000 each. In the event I received the £4,000 as gifts and the new manse was paid for and that was one thing less to be anxious about. It has been my experience that when there is a worthwhile goal, people will give generously. It was so for our new church. One pensioner from time to time would give me a hundred pound notes in an envelope but wished to remain anonymous. I thanked the Lord for the generosity of so many.

Over two hundred people gathered on Saturday 10th January 1981, on a bitter winter's afternoon, for the stone laying. Mrs

God so loved.........that He gave..........

John 3:16

Seaton Methodist Church

Stanfield, whose husband John some years earlier had the vision of a new church, laid the foundation stone. Her late husband in his retirement carried out an amazing ministry at Colyford, that brought a small village to the point of needing a new and larger church. John and May Stanfield spent all their lives in China, working there as missionaries until their retirement. The ceremony was also used to launch her book, published by Epworth Press, entitled: *From Manchu to Mao*, which in a series of letters told of their life as missionaries. The book sold for £3.25, and the proceeds went towards the church funds. We sang the hymn "Christ is the foundation", and the Reverend Amos Cresswell, chairman of the Plymouth and Exeter District, gave the address. After the hymn "Blessed City, heavenly Salem" and the thanks and blessing, a queue formed to lay bricks at £1 a time. Over 100 of those present, including members of the local churches, Rotarians, and Seaton Town Councillors, laid bricks, raising £146. After the ceremony we all adjourned for refreshments in the St. John's Ambulance Hall where Mrs May Stanfield, 95 years of age, signed copies of her book.

At a press conference I read out a statement of the aim of our new church as follows: "Our aim is to provide a church for the people of

153

the community which is attractive and conducive for Christian worship, to be a centre for growth in Christian living, to be outgoing in a ministry of loving and caring."

The foundation stone had been truly laid, and by the end of January 1981 the walls of the church had risen to ten feet high. The one-acre plot began to take shape and the money poured in. On reading the story of the rebuilding of the walls of Jerusalem, vividly told in the memoirs of Nehemiah, I couldn't help thinking of my congregation when I read: "So we built the walls because the people had a mind to work". Even before work had officially commenced on the site members of the congregation took wheelbarrows and in relays worked over the ground, collecting up all the stones. The old chapel at Colyford was sold for £10,000. The Reverend Clifford Bell, residing at the time in Plymouth, sent from his churches advance fund the sum of £2,500 and a good friend, Reverend Dr Richard Jones, sent from his district the sum of £3,000. An elderly lady in the church promised upon her death the sum of £30,000 and there would be more to come on the death of her sister, also quite elderly, and so the money continued to flow in from many parts of the circuit in direct gifts and interest-free loans, but there were still problems to overcome.

One morning I was called to the site when the church, the hall and two rooms and a kitchen were well on the way to being built, but there was sufficient land left to build three extra rooms, a small hall, another kitchen, and two toilets. The decision had to be made on the spot. There was no time to call a circuit meeting. Had we called a halt to the extension of the scheme we were fairly certain the extra accommodation would never have been possible to build at a later date because of the cost. I wondered what I should do as there had already been some opposition to the scheme by some members of the circuit meeting, mainly on the question of finance. The extra building would cost at least £40,000, and what would the bank manager have to say to that? From the site caravan I telephoned Peter Kerridge, the Divisional Property Secretary at Manchester, and he promptly told me to go ahead and the bonus was that he promised a further ten per cent gift on the monies raised locally. We were to have a complete set of buildings, all that we needed, and so the work proceeded. The

Interior of the church

workmen were racing against time so that the church could be opened and dedicated on Saturday the 26th September 1981.

The night before the opening was due to take place lots of members and friends put in the finishing touches, arranged flowers and made the sanctuary beautiful. I stood outside the church where an enormous cross had been erected, and I felt proud to be minister of this new church. I knew it would be a success.

The day for the opening had come at last and a congregation of five hundred people gathered in the new church. I stood at the entrance and at precisely three o'clock I knocked at the door and said, "Open to me the gates of righteousness: I will go in to them, and I will praise the Lord." The doors were unlocked by Mr Paul Bartlett Lang, after he had received the key from the architect, Mr Francis Bush, ARIBA. Mr Paul Bartlett Lang then delivered the key to me and said, "In the name of the Father and the Son and of the Holy Spirit I declare this building open and deliver to you the key thereof. I pray you now to dedicate it for the use of the Methodist Church in the worship of Almighty God." I then replied, "I accept this key in token of the trust committed to the Methodist Church in Seaton." I then invited Mrs Stanfield to unveil the plaque that recorded the grateful thanks of the church to the Joseph Rank Benevolent Trust for their generous grant given toward the building of the church. After the plaque had been dedicated I said, "We are ready to proceed to the dedication. Peace be to this house and all who worship therein. Peace be to those who enter, and to those who go out therefrom. Peace be to those who love it, and love the name of the Lord Jesus Christ." As the ministers and lay people processed into the church the congregation sang the hymn "Praise my soul the king of Heaven". Prayers were said and then the first lesson was read by Mr Henry Davis and Mr Alan Stevens. An act of dedication was conducted by the Chairman of the Exeter and Plymouth District. The congregation said, "Compassed by a great cloud of witnesses, grateful for our heritage, sensible of the sacrifice of our fathers in the faith, confessing that apart from us their work cannot be made perfect, we dedicate ourselves anew to the worship and service of Almighty God." Each minister then in turn read a Bible passage at the font, the pulpit, the communion rail and at the cross. After the singing of the hymn "The head that once was crowned with thorns", the Reverend Amos Cresswell, MA, preached the sermon, powerful in proclamation, challenging and inspiring.

The opening and dedication of our new church was a memorable occasion. But it was only the beginning, for there was the task of building up the church, and this was accomplished through the prayers, work, and faith of a band of dedicated people. Within a few years of opening the membership had grown from seventy to 120 members. A choir was established and an introit and anthem sung at every act of morning worship. A Bible class was started that, with fervent prayer, became the powerhouse of the church. It was also open to other churches in the town. It was in the Bible class study group that I met a lady from the Anglican church, whose step-grandfather was Godfrey Thring, a Prebendary of Wells Cathedral, with Matthew Bridges writer of the hymn: "Crown him with many crowns". She became our friend, sharing in the joy of Christian fellowship, and by her dedicated life and generous gifts strongly supported our work and ministry.

In the early summer of 1982 our daughter Jane began making plans for her marriage, and on Wednesday 28th July I had the joy and privilege of marrying her in our Codsall church to Trevor

Jane's wedding

Lucy's baptism

Starling. It was a memorable day. I amused the relatives and friends at the reception when I told them that her mother's maiden name was Bird, and Jane had married a Starling!. They settled down well to married life, and on Friday 4th July 1986 Jane gave birth to a daughter, and so we became proud grandparents. She was named Lucy, and true to her name she brought light into the world for us. I also celebrated forty years in the active ministry and a special celebration was held in our Seaton church when greetings were read our from each of the churches in which Betty and I had served. My last few years at Seaton went quickly and retirement meant moving from Seaton to Sidmouth, where we bought a bungalow in a pleasant part called Woolbrook.

The Methodist Church calls its retired ministers by the name of "supernumeraries", a title meaning surplus to establishment. It really is a misnomer for many retired ministers give devoted service during

"Treetops", our bungalow

their retirement. One of the highlights in the Ministerial session of the District Synod was the moment when the names of those becoming supernumeraries were read out. Tributes of almost unqualified praise were given by ministers who knew them, worked with them, or were grateful to God for their friendship and ministry, The replies of retiring ministers often brought much laughter, but there were moments of serious reflection when they gave some of the highlights of their ministry.

Chapter Eighteen

Retirement

The day came in May 1987 for me to ask permission to retire from the active ministry. It was with mixed feelings that I made my request; today in the active ministry with responsibilities as pastor of a flock, tomorrow a supernumerary minister, with no special flock to care for, no meetings to chair, and only the occasional baptism, wedding, and funeral at which to officiate. But forty-one years were long enough to be in the active ministry; as Dean Inge wrote, "It is far wiser to retire before the inevitable decline of one's powers become manifest to the outside world". But what does it mean to retire? Dr Alex Vidler, an Anglican priest, after two years of retirement wrote:

> Already for two years I have been blessedly retired, and am one of those people who not only looked forward to retirement, but who believed in retiring, who believed, that is to say, in detaching oneself, so far as possible from one's previous responsibilities, interests and concerns and embracing new ones, or in cultivating employments that have hitherto been able to occupy only a marginal place in one's life. Thus I make no attempt now to follow the course of theological debates or ecclesiastical affairs, as I used to do, still less to intervene in them. I am perfectly content to leave others the arena in which at one time I sought to exert a modest influence, or at any rate to utter an occasional word or two.

I found I agreed largely with the spirit of those words, but I trusted that though many wished to live having escaped notice, the Church everywhere would continue to value the presence and service of retired ministers and that no one retiring would feel redundant. Perhaps one should take notice of the wise advice of the poet Goethe, who wrote: "Above all, no reproaches about what is past and cannot be altered. Look backward with gratitude. Look forward with hope. Look upward with confidence".

For several months after retirement I felt I was on a "sabbatical" until it dawned on me that it was going to go on and on. I simply had to have a daily programme. I found an increasing joy in making sermons and preaching them and painting in a range of mediums, oils, watercolors, acrylics, pastels and gouache. I had my first one man exhibition, when I was able to show over one hundred paintings, some which I had painted over forty years ago. However, I still wanted to follow a course of studies and found interest in reading each month the *Expository Times*, a splendid journal to keep my mind fresh and alert in all matters affecting Bible study and preaching.

During my probationary studies I was required to study New Testament Greek and found it difficult. However, I was determined to master it, and found my enthusiasm for the subject increased. I applied to the External Registrar at London University to read for the degree of Bachelor of Divinity. I was almost seventy-four, but looked forward to the challenge. The standard for the this degree was the same as that of internal candidates on a full-time basis. The degree covered a wide field of study; New Testament Greek; Old Testament: Israel and the Great Powers; Christian Doctrine; Church History; Philosophy of Religion; and a choice of other subjects from which I selected Christian Ethics and Romans in Greek. I found it necessary to do at least fifteen hours study a week for three years. It was required of external students to go to London University Examination Halls to take written examinations, usually in May of each year. I did this for three years, completing altogether thirty-three hours of written examinations. I remember that on the first occasion I attended for the examinations I saw lots of students outside the examination halls doing last-minute revision. I recall hearing one young lady exclaim to her friend, "It's coming to something when grandfathers sit for examinations!" Of course, it's not unusual these days for the retired to sit for degrees. The only snag was that it cost over £3,000 to complete the three-year studies, providing fees, books, and travelling to and staying in London at The Penn Club, a Quaker establishment, but it was worth it.

I enjoyed my visits to London. One day I took the opportunity of walking through Lincoln's Inn Fields where, as a young man before the war, I often walked. The office where I first worked had been taken over by a bank, but memories came flooding back to me and I wondered what had happened to other members of the staff and what direction their lives had taken.

A "red letter day" after I had completed the degree was the presentation of graduates at the Barbican Centre in London in the presence of Her Royal Highness, the Princess Royal, Chancellor of the University of London. The ceremony marked the culmination of years of study on the part of graduates and the years of support given by members of families and friends. On this occasion there were only two Theology graduates, myself and a young lady. I bowed as I was presented and the Princess said: "Well done"; there rang out warm applause from the full auditorium of graduates, relatives and friends. The years of study had proved worthwhile, not just for the degree, but for the desire to go on learning. I recall that T. H. Green, the historian, had placed on his tombstone the words: "He died learning". What a splendid epitaph!

When I finished the degree studies I decided to hold a monthly Bible class. All through my ministry I held Bible classes, and so in retirement I started a Bible class that I called: "Sixty-minute Bible studies". Thirteen people from our church met each month in our lounge, and after coffee got down to the study of God's word. The class was on its seventh year and going strong. A. N. Wilson, in his challenging book *God's Funeral*, began with the sentence: "The God question does not go away". I believe it will never go away as long as people gather together, become a searching group, who in their search belong to, as *Michael Polanyi*, by Drusilla Scott, 1996, puts it, "A society of explorers".

There were a number of things we discovered as a group, chiefly that whatever book we looked at in the Bible offered an opportunity for fresh perspectives, so we discovered God's will for his church and for members of his church It gave a higher sense of personal identity and vocation. In these studies we tried to celebrate light, not darkness, and conviviality, not gloom. The time of study was precious, for it exposed the real spiritual and cultural ills from which we all suffer, and revealed God in Christ Jesus, who loved humanity so much that he chose to come to earth as an infant, buffeted by social circumstances and tribulations.

The years seemed to have passed by so quickly and my retirement so far has been full of interesting things, It was something of a surprise to me that when I started writing this autobiography I was past seventy-eight. When I entered the Methodist ministry I was twenty-three, now I have turned eighty. I have had a pretty good innings and a full and satisfying ministry, blessed with a wife who has been supportive and kindness itself.

As one grows, hopefully, in wisdom and knowledge, then one is bound to ask questions about the more intellectual side of faith over and above the more personal side. Was Jesus really born of a virgin, did he have two natures, human and divine, did he perform miracles, and did he really rise again from the dead? And, of course, many other questions.

Early in my Christian pilgrimage, which began in my Sunday School days, now so long ago, I learned by heart the Apostles' Creed, but this baptismal statement of faith dating back to the second century formed, as it were, only a basic structure of belief. I soon discovered that it was only through struggle from one pattern of thought to another that steadfast, unshakeable belief was wrought through the crucible of doubt. Whereas one is ready to take things at face value as a child, it is only as life unfolds, through all its changing scenes of trouble and joy, that one arrives at a firm, unshakeable faith that stands the test of time. I believe in God, not just because my mother taught me to say: "Our Father, who art in heaven", but because all my life I have tried to make sense of things, such as who am I, why was I born, where am I going? Later in my study of religious philosophy I looked more closely at the "Puzzle of God" and sought to find an answer to those questions. Enoch Powell, a well known politician, wrote a book called *No Easy Answers*, and in correspondence with him he spoke about the New Testament, which he affirmed contained endless puzzles. Nevertheless, he spent a lifetime endeavouring to find satisfactory answers and died still in search of them, but as one who believed in God.

Our existence is embraced by an ineffable mystery we call God. Try as we may to fathom this mystery, as I have tried again and again to do, I end each time by saying: "He is there". But how do I know that he is there? I can only say I know, just as Job in the Old Testament book by that name, despite all his suffering said: "I know that my Redeemer lives".

Yes, I believe in God and I believe in the one who helps me to believe in God, indeed convinces me in spite of all my questioning that God is there in Jesus. And so I can say: "I believe in Jesus"; as G. A. Studdert-Kennedy, a chaplain of the First World War said: "He is the portrait of the unseen God".

Now I've turned eighty, I realize that although I haven't got the same steam as I used to have I can still preach, paint and write. The computer entered my daily life and kept me busy some of the time, but like many of my age I expected some waning of my physical and mental powers.

A most devastating shock I had was when my immensely kind doctor thought I had prostate cancer and referred me to a urological specialist. Her provisional diagnosis was confirmed after I had a blood test called a PSA. The specialist confirmed after his examination that it was locally advanced cancer and that he didn't require me to have a biopsy.

The treatment for the first six months advised by my consultant was "Watching and waiting", which made me smile as one of our well known hymns; "Blessed assurance, Jesus is mine", had the line in the third verse "Watching and waiting, looking above". Fortunately a bone scan revealed all was clear, but my consultant said it was necessary to have special medication every day. My dear wife, family and friends gave me all the support I needed and my brother Stanley, said, "This will enrich your ministry"; it most certainly has and with faith it will continue to enrich it. All of this has turned my thoughts more than ever to the last great adventure – death. I ponder over this deeply but of course I have no idea when God will call me into the new life of heaven. However, as I approach the throne of the ineffable, I do so with confidence that God, who has blessed and guided me all through my life, will be in that heaven of heavens to give me a welcome when I die. I often think of heaven and what it will be like. When we sing the Christmas carol "Once in Royal David's City", we sing the words "He came down to earth from heaven". In Sunday School I used to sing: "There's a friend for little children above the bright blue sky". But we no longer think of heaven as being above, nor indeed of hell as being below. We all have our idea of heaven as being something somewhere, or nowhere; words cannot describe heaven but we think of it as being wonderful beyond our imagination. Language cannot describe the idea of heaven any more than it can describe the idea of God. Spatiality is by no means an essential of heaven. However, I believe in heaven and seldom a day goes by without thoughts of heaven, and when I do think about it I think of life after death because Jesus was raised by God from being dead, and so it shall be in our case too. I do not believe in the "maybe" of it, but in the certainty of it. We in the church speak of the "Christian hope" when we think of life after death, which, if nothing else, makes sense of our life here. It is interesting to note that the word "hope" does not appear either as a verb or a noun in the Book of Revelation, because it is a story of a man whose hope was all but extinguished but then kindled into a flame of living belief when he saw the risen Christ. The Bible teaches us that God is the God of the living, not of the dead. Resurrection faith is as simple as that. Jesus affirms resurrection because he arose from the dead. Every time I take a funeral I read aloud the sentence: "'I am the resurrection and the life', says the Lord. 'Those who believe in me, even though they die, will live, and everyone who lives and believes in me will never die'."

In our house we have a grandfather clock that is over two hundred years old, a miracle of survival. Someone in the family etched with a diamond on the glass face the words "God is love". I look at this text every night when I wind up the clock; it serves as a reminder that because God is love he will not cease to love me when I die. Indeed, what could I make of the love of God if at death he ceased to love me? Because he loves me now, he will love me when I leave this world, for his is a love that never ends, and nothing can separate me from the love of God, not even death.

I believe that when I pass through the last door that I shall ever pass through I shall see the face of God, but it will actually be the face of Jesus, whom I shall recognize immediately. And I shall be with Christ as he promised the robber hanging beside him when he said, "This day you will be with me in paradise", and it will be wonderful. beyond all our wildest dreams because we shall see again those we loved and lost a while, our parents, loved ones and friends, and we shall know them in a new light where forgiveness for wrongs done will make heaven the true blessing that God intends it to be. Someone who reads this may say: "I will need unlimited faith to believe all this". And my reply would be, "Yes, you will, but God is waiting right now to give you this kind of faith. Trust him."

We all need something or someone to believe in. Jesus Christ invites us to believe in God. I have found the following creed used in one of the principal churches in Ottawa most helpful.

I believe in a God of creation
who paints our earth with the colours of the rainbow,
who thunders in a cloudburst and whispers in a breeze,
who springs forth in the dawn and shines glorious in the sunset,
who dances at a baby's birth and rejoices in all things new.
I believe in a God who comes in the stillness of the night,
who enters the manger of our lives,
who walks beside us on the dusty roads of our journey,
who sets banquets to satisfy our hunger,
who triumphs over the trials we encounter,
who rolls away the stones which imprison us,
who rises in glory through the darkness which surrounds us,
whose only language is love.

I believe in a God who graces our lives,
who comforts our sorrows,
who stirs our hearts to respond in deeds of love,
who binds us to one another in peace,
whose Spirit fills the whole world.

And I would add to this splendid creed a final line:

I believe in Jesus Christ, who makes God real.

Being committed to Christ is no easy option, no insipid humdrum monotony, but the most fascinating and exciting adventure the human spirit can know. There are signs that the age is ripe for a great return to Christ, the Word made flesh.

One scholar who has made Christ real to me is Albert Schweitzer. He is well known in theological circles; some would say he was a many-sided genius, having obtained doctorates in philosophy, theology and music before he was thirty and later added a doctorate in medicine. But theologians will remember him for his book *The Quest of the Historical Jesus*, which caused a great stir among theologians for his interpretation and thought on the life of Jesus that allowed him to remain a man of his own day and culture. Schweitzer was a man of immense loving kindness, shown chiefly in his building the hospital in Lambarene and his lifelong devotion within the hospital to the healing ministry and to the "reverence for life", all of which came as a result of his love of Jesus. When he was a student he had above his desk in Gunsbach a modestly framed copy of a hymn, eloquent of the fervent idealism that was already the mark of his nature.

Higher, ever higher,
With your dreams and your desires,
Higher, ever higher,
The ideal you long to serve.
Higher, ever higher,
When the clouds begin to gather,

Higher, ever higher,
By the starlight of your faith.

Undoubtedly this hymn influenced the studious Albert and perhaps, with thoughts of Jesus in the indefatigable curiosity of his mind and his passion for knowledge, led him at the close of *The Quest of the Historical Jesus* to put in a heart- and mind-stunning paragraph, words which have gripped me so many times in my ministry and brought me face to face with the living Christ:

> He came to us as One unknown, without a name as of old, by the lakeside. He speaks to us the same words: "Follow me", and sets us to the task which he has to fulfill for our time. He commands. And to those who obey him, whether they be wise or simple, he will reveal himself in the toils, the conflicts the sufferings which they shall pass through in his fellowship, and, as an ineffable mystery, they shall learn in their own experience who he is.

The story of my life has been a life greatly influenced by my encounter with Jesus in those early days of the last war. What would have happened to me had I not had that encounter I do not know, but I do know that from that moment my main purpose was to seek God, and I knew that it would be a lifelong task, that the Church of Jesus Christ would be my spiritual centre, and that life would mean a daily turning of my heart and mind to God and to follow the way of Christ. When I met Jesus Christ it was as if he gave me a map for life, pointing clearly the way I should go. I have been singularly fortunate in having married Betty, who has shared to the full my ministry and, through her support and encouragement, made ministry a joy. I have endeavoured to preach Christ throughout my ministry and I hope to continue to do this.

Sir Walter Scott spoke about growing old as "going down the other side of the hill". I don't think of myself as growing old; indeed, apart from those aches and pains that so many experience, I still feel young within. Yes, there are the daily pills to take, and the visit to my doctor whose medical care I appreciate so much, but life is good and still full of interest, opportunity and challenge, and, as I see it, truly wonderful.

The whole of my life has been lived in the fellowship of the church. I have met many wonderful Christians whose lives have radiated the presence of Christ and helped me to grow in faith. Their witness has made me realize that my purpose has been to bring Jesus to others, and to take his tenderness and love to each soul I have been privileged to meet. There can be no greater privilege and responsibility. Whatever I have been able to accomplish has been because of the grace of Christ and those who have encouraged me and shared in making visions come true.

How time flies. One becomes aware of this as each year passes; how the days dwindle down so quickly, there's so much to do and such a little time, it would seem, to do all those things that fascinate the mind and imagination. Growing old must not be regarded simply as time running out but as part of God's eternal plan, part of the map of life. I don't look forward to dying but I do look forward to the "last great adventure", death, for which the whole of life has been a preparation. I do not know what it will be like but I believe that life will go on in a new dimension, and that it will be one of ecstasy and complete happiness.

There is a sense in which an autobiography can never be finished. So long as we are alive there is always something else to follow. My life has been full of interest and I believe that every future day will have something of interest and perhaps even of excitement. Like Moses, I have been to the mountain top and looked over, and I have seen the promised land. I don't know at what stage I will get the call to enter but when it comes I am sure it will be the greatest adventure of all and the new world will be before me and Christ will be there, and when "the evening comes and the fever of life is over and my work is done", in Immanuel's land I shall see him face to face, the King in his beauty. What more could I ask? God has given me all I need. *Soli Deo Gloria*! "To God alone, the glory".

Epilogue

I believe that faith is a task for a lifetime and the highest passion a human being can experience. Coming to faith meant starting a journey of adventure. Looking back I know I could not have survived the difficult times without faith. The church was the vehicle through which Jesus first made this faith known to me, and I will always love Jesus and his church. But it makes me sad to think that many live outside the church, and sadder still, without Jesus. And so I ask, what is the future of the church? Karl Barth said, "it is God's provisional demonstration for all humanity." If this is true, and I believe that it is, I ask, what is the church supposed to do? It is my firm conviction that the church exists to evangelize the world, to train boys and girls, men and women, in Christian character, to worship and praise God, and witness to those lofty ideals upon which alone human happiness and security depend. But most of all I believe that it is to commend Jesus as the Saviour of the world.

I am aware that other faiths teach high and noble standards of belief, and we need to understand this.

It is my prayer that the ideas, thoughts, and experiences on my journey of faith will be of interest and encouragement to other souls.

Closing Prayer

The lights of evening grace the sky,
The moon and stars in brightness shine;
But Christ is more than light on high,
Christ is the light which outstrips time.

Christ is the light which leads and guides,
through all the winding paths of life;
To show the way of righteousness,
The goal to reach when facing strife.

Christ is the light which ever shines
As pure light upon our way;
Piercing the darkness of the night
To show the way for each new day.

Christ is the light to challenge all
New paths to show the way to go;
From his great store of wondrous grace,
Enough to face whatever foe.

Christ is the light which judges all,
Through each new day, through every hour;
Bending each will to do the right,
Giving his strength and awesome power.

O Christ the light of all the world,
The heart of all that's good and true;
Reach out to all who need you now,
And in your love make all things new.

Metre L. M. Tune: Martham

INDEX